Praise for *The Rise*

"My friend Danette shares her transformational story with courage, love, and vulnerability. She has handled loss, trauma, and hardship with incredible grace and created a life beyond her wildest dreams. Danette will inspire you to rise up, heal old wounds, and live with radical authenticity and freedom!"

— **Gabrielle Bernstein**, #1 *New York Times* best-selling author of *The Universe Has Your Back*

"*The Rise* is one of the most inspiring, deeply moving, and motivational books I've read. It reminds us of the power we each have to turn our pain into purpose and use our lowest points as a springboard to reach our highest potential. If you're ready to rise, let Danette be your loving guide and fierce champion. She's absolutely brilliant."

— **Kris Carr**, *New York Times* best-selling author of *Crazy Sexy Juice*

"I love Danette May and her latest book, *The Rise*. It is an inspiring guide for all women who are ready to rise up and lead."

— **Rebecca Campbell**, world-renowned artist, creative, and best-selling author of *Rise Sister Rise* and *Light Is the New Black*

"Danette May is a gifted storyteller who shows us the way to overcome obstacles and rise above life's darkest moments. By sharing her traumatic journey of unimaginable loss and taking us step by step through the process of putting her life back together again, we learn the power of resilience."

— **Kathy Smith**, fitness icon and *New York Times* best-selling author of *Feed Muscle, Shrink Fat Diet*

"Real transformation is what happens when someone decides to listen to their soul no matter the consequences. Danette is a warrior of truth-telling and truthful living."

— **Lori Harder**, top 100 podcast host, transformational coach, fitness world champion, and best-selling author of *A Tribe Called Bliss*

"An inspiring, beautiful, and courageous book that calls us to examine our own stories and struggles, in order to turn our breakdowns into our biggest breakthroughs."

— **Alexi Panos**, transformational teacher, humanitarian, and author of *Now or Never*

"*The Rise* is a courageous, raw, and brilliant story of how to use some of the most shattering circumstances in life to transform into our highest selves. Danette May dives into her vulnerability and takes every opportunity to turn fear and pain into love and light, which she then tirelessly shares with the world."

— **Lindsay Sukornyk**, transformational coach

"*The Rise* is much more than a book . . . it is a beautifully written invitation into self-discovery and personal transformation. It is through Danette's authenticity and vulnerability that she shares her story, her truth, and invites us into a process to discover and honor our own."

— **Maya Comerota Stewart**, transformational coach and founder of 528HzInc

The Rise

The Rise

An Unforgettable Journey of Self-Love,
Forgiveness, and Transformation

DANETTE MAY

HAY HOUSE, INC.
Carlsbad, California • New York City
London • Sydney • New Delhi

Copyright © 2018 by Danette May

Published in the United States by: Hay House, Inc.: www.hayhouse
.com® • **Published in Australia by:** Hay House Australia Pty. Ltd.:
www.hayhouse.com.au • **Published in the United Kingdom by:**
Hay House UK, Ltd.: www.hayhouse.co.uk • **Published in India by:**
Hay House Publishers India: www.hayhouse.co.in

Interior design: Nick C. Welch

**Cataloging-in-Publication Data is on file
with the Library of Congress**

Hardcover ISBN: 978-1-4019-5618-9
E-book ISBN: 978-1-4019-5619-6
Audiobook ISBN: 978-1-4019-5620-2

10 9 8 7 6 5 4 3 2 1
1st edition, October 2018

Printed in the United States of America

*This book is dedicated to every woman who
wonders if she matters and deep down knows
she does. To all the women who are ready to use
their voice, to stand on their stories, to remember
on a cellular soul level that it is time to Rise into
the fullest expression of who we are!
Let's unite. Let's Love Fiercely one another and
most importantly ourselves. It's Time to Rise.*

CONTENTS

Dear Friend,

Before you dive in, I do want to give you a warning. The stories in these pages are *raw* and may cause you to look at your life differently.

This is not your typical self-help book. It is more of a personal disruption book that will make you rethink aspects of your life that may have been running on cruise control for years.

Within months, maybe weeks, of reading this book, you may find yourself no longer accepting certain aspects of your life. You will start to look at your relationships, your finances, your day-to-day decisions, and your goals differently. You may find that the things you have been tolerating no longer align with the truth of your soul.

You will take a deep look at the stories you tell yourself every day—both your past choices and current reality. This book is designed to awaken the powerful, conscious, impactful human and spiritual being that your soul is asking to come forth.

As I share my story, it is my hope that you will find yours within it. I hope to empower you to reevaluate, recalibrate, take ownership, and, most importantly, celebrate your life. You may begin to see what you do not want to see, but for us to grow, we must become vulnerable and willing to look at ourselves and our lives from a different vantage point.

Throughout the book, certain foods or meals I ate, movements I did, or mindset practices that took me to the next level are marked by an asterisk [*]. Visit www.Rise Gifts .com or see the Resources section at the back of the book for free access to the tools that I used in my own Rise.

Since this book is about using your voice, standing on top of your stories, and creating a life by your design, I created a platform where we can come together to share our stories, grow into our fullest expression, and connect on a deeper level. I will not let you hide alone. It's time to come together. Refer to the Resources section and join me and your fellow readers online.

I love being in touch with you. I love hearing your stories and linking arms.

Your sister in the Rise,
Danette

INTRODUCTION

There is no greater agony than bearing an untold story inside you.

— MAYA ANGELOU

My hands shake, my stomach is in knots, and my neck rages with acne and blemishes. My soul has asked me to write about my mud, my muck, my stories that I didn't want anyone to know. Why? That's a question I have asked my soul over and over, especially at 2 A.M. when the anxiety sweeps over my body, crawling up my chest, and covering my face. These are my stories, these are my hidden moments of chaos, my lowest of lows and my highest of highs.

Why must I write these stories?

Will I be accepted if I lay it all out on the line?

Will my parents and my ex-husband see why I shared the darkness of the past?

Will they understand that it's so we can see that light can win every time?

How will my daughters take these truths about their mother?

My mind races and my ego chimes in . . .

All the forgiveness you have reached will vanish if you share these stories.

Your daughters will see your weaknesses and forget your strengths.

You are shaming your family.

No one wants to read your story.

You will be judged.

My soul shouts, trying its hardest to drown out the ego of my mind. It knows that I am in new territory. It knows I have never shared some of these stories. It knows how vulnerable I am, sharing these deepest secrets. It *knows* what is coming.

What my soul knows and what I know is this: For centuries women and men have been afraid to stand naked in their truth. They have been afraid to share their shame, their pain, their wrongdoings, and their beliefs—for fear of being shunned. Because what if they lay their hearts bare, and no one hears, or cares, or makes a shift for the better—then what?

Our world is filled with an immense amount of abundance, of love and forgiveness. But a cloud of separation still looms.

We have come such a long way, but there is still evidence of hatred, of separation. We remain divided culturally and religiously because our belief systems aren't quite aligned. And so various races, countries, communities, men, and women are walking around, shoving down their stories and their vulnerability as if they are separate, alone in their pain, their lives, and their stories.

My soul knows that one of the first profound steps in healing is sharing the ugly, raw, messy truth. Using our voice of love, our voice for change. When I say *sharing*, I don't mean the type of sharing where you sit around and share and everyone feels sorry for you and you get to wallow in your story. You don't get to play the victim, the "woe is me" card. That's not sharing; that's stirring the pot. That's staying in your story.

It's time we Stand on our Stories! It's time we use them as stepping-stones to our Rise. And as we share, and as we heal individually, and as we choose *love* and *forgiveness* every time, we as a collective can Rise. Rise to a new way of living, loving, and truly healing this planet.

I knew that I couldn't be the *only* one who doesn't want to share the real messy parts of my life—because I know we *all* have messy parts. I also know that our truth is simply that—our truth. It doesn't mean it is *The Truth*. We can only experience life from the perspective of our pain. We can take the same experience and see it totally differently, based on our early childhood experiences, on past triggers and past emotions. And once we share, we can start to bridge the gap of separation and start healing.

As we share, we can see a common thread that is weaved through all mankind. *We all love* deeply, and *we all want to be loved* deeply. We are all doing our best with where we are. *We are all connected.* And we all want to be in full expression of our soul's purpose.

This is my story and my truth.

My truth of being untruthful.

My truth of anger, sadness, and not feeling enough.

My truth of once wanting to die to now waking up each day before my alarm, excited for life.

My truth of vibing high and then within 30 minutes feeling like no one sees me.

My truth that I am 100 percent responsible for what has happened and will happen in my life.

My truth of doing the work, especially when I don't feel like it.

My truth that each life is divine, and that energy, unseen forces, and angels do exist.

I share my story and my truth in hopes that you will share *your story*. That you will own your responsibility for that story, and then stand on it through forgiveness, through choosing your power and *love* over all else.

At the end of each section, I have highlighted the insights I have received through my mud, my mess, my growth. These insights are purely my opinion, my truth. In my story, I hope you will find yours.

I am blessed to live an amazing and adventurous life! I am the founder of Mindful Health, LLC; creator of The Rise movement; and author of the best-selling books *Eat, Drink, and Shrink*; *7 Day Jumpstart*; and *Bikini Body Detox*. As a motivational speaker and celebrity trainer, I've helped millions of people learn to live healthier lives, feel better, and gain more energy. I have a passion and mission beating in my heart to empower women through the foundation of healing movement, healing foods, and a healing mind-set, and I am fueled by this mission every single day. I've included some free online resources to help you in your journey at the end of the book. They are marked by an asterisk (*) throughout so that you know to look them up later at risegifts.com.

I'm a mother of two daughters, and these two future women are my priority and my gift. I am dedicated to growing to my full potential so that I can show them that they can do the same. I want them to have the confidence and beliefs necessary to pursue their dreams. I want them to have determination to overcome any obstacles. And above all, I want them to know without a shred of doubt that they are loved and have great worth, no matter what they do or do not do in this world. That they are loved simply because they exist.

I know that it can feel like you're living the *wrong life*. I felt that way.

Do you feel the life you're living isn't the one you're meant for—that there's something greater pulling at your heart—that there is a higher calling? *Listen to that.* I want you to learn to expand beyond what you ever thought possible, because the result is a sense of radical self-love, belief, and manifestation that knows no bounds.

This journey isn't unique to me—or to you! This journey is for all of us. This is the Rise of the wild, loving, connected, accepting, and openhearted woman!

This is a time when people are linking arms to create change. Women around the world are uncovering old wounds, casting off limitations, and letting go of shame and rejection in order to heal. It is through this individual healing that we will heal the wounds in our communities, in our cultures, and ultimately the planet.

I invite you to join me in this movement, as we link arms and hearts with women all over the world. Together we can empower each other as we discover our soul's purpose, find our voice, step into our power, and live an authentic life. Together, we Rise.

The New Way

We are at the dawn of a new era

A new way of living

Where love is our religion

Forgiveness, our currency

And. Every. Single. Person.

Knows that they matter.

There is a new tribe of women

Who have heard the call

And have agreed on a soul level

To unite at this time in history.

Women who are ready

To shift their mind-set

To break down the walls

To shatter paradigms

To adopt this new way.

Women who are ready

To stand in their power

To own their voice

To tell their story

And to speak their truth.

Women who are committed to

Fiercely and passionately loving themselves

And all of their dimensions.

Women who have a deep knowing that

We. Are. All. One.

That I am you and you are me

And that together, we will Rise.

This is beyond feminism

This is beyond you

This is beyond me

This is equanimity

And *this* is a higher calling.

It is a new way

Of living

Of loving

Of seeing the world.

And this new way

will heal the planet.

This is a call to action to women worldwide.

Can you hear it?

Today is the day to answer the call.

It is time to stand up

It is time to link arms

It is time to unite

It is time . . . to RISE.

CHAPTER 1

Radical Truth-Telling

Speaking your truth is the most
powerful tool we all have.

— OPRAH WINFREY

At the age of 22, I found myself inexplicably sobbing in my car, parked on a tree-lined street at Utah State University. As I walked out of my last class of the evening, I knew the breakdown was coming—I could feel the rage boiling in my stomach, my hands tingling with anxious energy. I knew I needed to get to a safe place immediately so I could erupt in private. But when you are a poor college student who lives in an apartment with your husband and there are paper-thin walls separating your apartment from those of the other students living all around you, you have to get creative.

I drove my old blue Nissan Altima to the base of a hill where people rarely parked. I wanted to be where no one would hear me or see me, because I couldn't give an explanation I wasn't even ready to give myself.

I'd been sledding down this hill; I'd even learned how to snowboard on it a few years earlier. It was the famous spot where couples gathered to stand on the college "A" sign, the symbol for the Utah State Aggies, and confirm their love with a kiss. And here I was, questioning everything I'd ever believed about life and love.

Shielded by tall trees on either side, and thankfully with no one else around, I let go. The noises that bellowed up from my stomach were shrill and harsh, extreme and desperate. It was the ugliest noise I had ever made, and I screamed and banged on the steering wheel. I was embarrassed at the intensity of my emotion—and I was in awe of my own capacity to release. It felt good to let it out.

I'd never had a breakdown like this. Not once. Even my childhood tantrums were extremely mild in comparison. No, I'd always been on my best behavior. I'd always done "the right thing." It was an unfortunate time to unravel, right on the verge of college graduation, right before our one-year wedding anniversary. And there I was, wondering how I got to this place, to this rage, to this situation, to being this girl I did not recognize. I wasn't sure how to get out.

It wasn't even like some specific terrible event had happened moments before. No one had said anything awful to me in class that made me burst into tears. I hadn't had a fight with my husband, either.

Nothing was wrong, really.

Yet, everything was wrong.

Not even one year into my marriage, I felt trapped in a life that was making me desperately unhappy and there was nothing I could do about it. After all, I'd still gone ahead with the wedding despite major doubts. Everyone said it was normal—the "cold feet" phenomenon. They said it would pass as soon as I said, "I do." But it hadn't.

A few weeks before the wedding, we'd gone to sign the legal papers at the county clerk's office at the courthouse. And, suddenly, I was terrified. I made my then-fiancé turn the car around, putting off the signatures until another day.

I did go back, and we did sign the papers. And then the morning of our wedding, we were at the temple of my church. I was getting ready, and I was shaking. My sister-in-law was helping me with my hair when I told her, "I am scared. I don't want to get married."

You know those feelings you get when you feel something is out of alignment, those guided intuitions? It's the turning in your belly, the tightness around your neck, the feeling like you want to throw up. The inner knowing that something is "off." I looked at my parents with all the seriousness I could gather in my soul and told them the same thing—I didn't want to get married.

"You are just nervous. Everyone feels this way," they said.

"Really? *Everyone* feels like they don't want to get married, but they do it anyway?"

Again, they told me it was nerves and I accepted it. And in the year since my wedding day, I told myself white lies—*stories*—every moment of every day.

To be fair, my husband wasn't a bad person at all; he genuinely was a nice guy. In fact, he was especially nice to me. He would tell me I was pretty; not just pretty, but the pretty that didn't require makeup. He would say I was a "natural beauty," and it always made me feel special. We didn't have a lot of money, so he would get creative on finding ways to have fun. Some of our favorite dates were picnics in the park and on the rooftop of our old rental home.

The reason I was able to have this breakdown in the first place was because he was supportive of me. It wasn't that I didn't love him. It wasn't that simple. Something deep down in my cells was screaming at me, telling me we were not meant to walk the rest of our lives together as husband and wife.

I felt there was a misalignment of our mission and paths. But divorce simply was not acceptable in my religion, and I didn't even consider it.

What's wrong with me? Why don't I love my life? Why am I feeling like this? I sat in my car, running out of Kleenex, running out of options.

At the time, my husband and I were in our last year of college. His degree was in business and mine was premed. Although I had always been fascinated with the human body, I didn't go on to be a doctor because as an M.D. I would see most of my patients *after* an illness or medical event occurred. I wanted to do preventative medicine, rather than reactive, so I became a nutritionist and personal trainer. That way I could help people with their body and with nutrition, hopefully preventing illness and unhealthy choices.

I had always loved school and had graduated high school with a 4.0 GPA. College was the same. I did everything right—I played all the sports, made all the grades, always sat in the front row at church, and had married an upstanding member of our community. *So why was this happening to me?*

I had felt an immense freedom when I left home and entered college. I could finally buy my own food, especially the foods I liked. I could eat on the couch and stay up late. I didn't have to make my bed or ask if I could visit friends. I could spend my money how I wanted to spend it. I was my own accountability.

And that sense of freedom had continued to develop over the course of my college years. And now, in my senior year, I was starting to realize that I was actually free— at least from the conservative upbringing of my youth, where the rules there were black and white. Now hundreds of miles away from home, they could be any color I chose, though I wasn't entirely sure what those were.

Here is what I did know:

I was married to a nice person.
I did not want to be married.
My soul was asking for more.

The thoughts that were coming to me were heavy and hard, screaming with urgency as they shot through my cells. The safety of my car allowed for a complete honest assessment. There was no one to judge me. No one to tell me I was wrong or to chastise me for thinking outside the lines.

Had I just *pretended* to be the perfect, holy religious girl?

Did I get married young to someone who was my friend for whom I had no passion, because I was afraid to be alone?

Did I marry the "nice" guy because my truth was that passion scared me?

I was angry at myself and angry about my life. I felt like I'd been lied to about sex, about marriage, about relationships. And I wished I'd listened to myself. *For once.*

With my breathing finally slowed and my body exhausted from the release, I thought back to when I was a little girl, when life was totally carefree. Back when my only responsibilities were barnyard chores and playing with animals.

Times of Tenderness: Growing Up on the Ranch

Salmon, Idaho, has a population of about 3,000 people. Our family—my parents, my four brothers, and I—lived in a small one-level house on a farm until I was 12. I learned how to work hard and to play hard.

Growing up with four brothers in a loving family in the country, I experienced true freedom where my imagination could go wild. There were mountains, rivers, and a stream in our front yard. Under the blue sky, I was innocent and carefree.

My room was a feminine oasis, away from the dirt and the boys. With matching carpet, bedspread, and wallpaper, I'd play with my Barbies or read, or listen to my record player for hours. Sometimes, if the weather was nice and after chores were done, I'd take my Barbies to the ditch in the front yard, where I would pretend we were camping or fantasize about what my life would look like when I was a grown-up.

For a while, we had a hundred sheep and four horses, and we always had between two and four dogs. Without a sister to play with or other kids within walking distance, these animals became my closest friends. Every day I would walk out into the pasture and see them. Sometimes I would sit on the railing and sing to the sheep and pretend they were my audience, happily listening to me. Every animal accepted me as I was. This was my oasis.

In the winter, we would get to watch the births. When a ewe went into labor, we would be on watch to go down and check on her. Even as a little kid, I knew I was going to witness either the miracle of birth or the sadness and heaviness of death.

One night, when I was quite young, my brother's sheep went into labor. We walked with flashlights down to the back pasture, passing the dog kennels and some of the chickens into the creaky, old barn. The ewe was struggling and breathing hard, and there was tension in the air because we knew the labor was going longer than usual. She was yelping out in pain, and we did all we could to pull the lamb from her body.

Just as the sun started to rise through the cracks of the barn, the lamb was finally extracted. I could hear the sweet little bellow of the lamb's voice. Sadly, the mom had struggled too long; it was just too hard of a labor, and she was slowly passing. This was my first experience with death. It was a sad time, but also a miraculous time. We needed to hurry, because as the ewe was dying, we had this brand-new baby that needed milk and nurturing immediately. I ran to the house in my big, oversize boots, because my brother Brett had already gone inside to get some breakfast—and perhaps to mourn a bit for his sheep, though he would never have admitted it. I didn't even take off my shoes before I chirped, "Can I have your baby lamb?!"

Brett looked up. Between spoonfuls of cereal, he said, "You have to take care of it and bottle-feed it, and I am not taking care of it for you."

I was perfectly happy with that deal, because all I wanted to do was take care of that baby lamb! I fell in love with the lamb that night and I was so excited because my brother had just confirmed that it could be *my lamb*. I would be responsible for another life! I knew it would be both exciting and tiring at times, and that it would demand a new level of responsibility and maturity I'd never had before.

I ran back down to the barn and told my parents, "Brett said this could be my lamb!"

My dad said, "Well, you better hurry up and get a bottle warmed up because this baby needs some food."

I got the bottle ready, but the baby lamb was not standing up. Usually lambs tend to stand up and start to walk, but he had just lost his mom. He was alone. He was afraid. He was exhausted and not doing very well. This was going to be my moment to take care of something that was only mine. I sat down on the ground in that barn in the straw and mud, surrounded with newborn matter. I took that lamb into my arms and started to glide the nipple into his mouth, and he started to eat.

I affectionately named him Joey. Every day, multiple times a day, I would run down and feed him. He soon imprinted on me, became my best friend, and truly thought I was his mom. He grew to be abnormally big, almost the size of a deer.

It was a big joke in town because no one had seen a sheep so big before. He was very skinny, but very tall, with unusually long legs. He didn't even act like a normal sheep. When he wanted to see me, he came to my back door and pounded on it with his hooves to have me come out. Then we would run through the fields and play together. All I had to do was run to the backyard, hold on to the fence rails, and yell, "Joey," and he would come running up to me.

At one point, I also had a duck that would follow me around the yard. My dad had found it on the side of the road when it was just a duckling. It imprinted on me and would follow me everywhere. I'd lie in our $10 plastic swimming pool from the dollar store and Willy the duck would sit on my belly as we glided in the water.

Sometimes I would put him on the slide and have him slide into the pool.

These were my friends. This was my childhood. These memories reminded me of when I felt free. I was so innocent and pure and full of life, until life tossed me face-first into the mud and the muck.

YOUNG LOVE

Twelve was an awkward age. It was the year I got my period and when my body started to change into a more feminine figure. My parents were trying to help me make the transition from little girl to young woman, but I didn't want to. I wanted to keep playing in the dirt. I didn't want to learn how to cook and sew and be a wife and mother someday.

I was raised in the Church of Jesus Christ of Latter-Day Saints (LDS), and an outsider looking in on that religion would say it was very strict. You were home by 10 o'clock. You didn't date until you were 16, and you usually only dated people in the religion. You only wore pants past your knees and no tank tops. You didn't show skin. *You certainly didn't wear a bikini.* When you did date, you *only* kissed and really, kissing should never be a French kiss, because that was sex in the mouth. And, of course, you waited until you were married for sex.

When I was 12, a young LDS boy named Jay liked me. He was my first love and the first boy I'd kissed. It all felt so perfect. He was such a kind person. He had a different way of thinking, and he acted different than the other boys. He never treated me poorly to try to show off to his friends.

After one of the many summer church trips we'd gone on together, I was sitting on the grass in front of the church, waiting for my parents to pick me up. It was a cool night, and the stars were out. Jay sat down next to me, held my hand, and told me how much he liked me. Holding hands felt so naughty and exciting. I instantly got butterflies—those sweet feelings that accompany a first crush. Then he leaned over and kissed me!

By that time, we were boyfriend and girlfriend and we had sent notes to each other after church and had long phone calls, both of us getting in trouble for talking longer than 10 minutes.

I knew we loved each other, inasmuch as children can be in love. But when school started in the fall, I decided I didn't want a boyfriend and I didn't want to be serious about a relationship. After all, I was only 12. So I used my voice and spoke my truth. I let Jay know that I was no longer his girlfriend.

This created massive turmoil for him on top of other things he was dealing with at that time—but I didn't know about any of his personal struggles. He sent me letter after letter, begging me to please take him back, swearing he'd be a better person—when I'd never thought he was anything less than a wonderful person.

As the letters progressed, I noticed a sense of anger. His rage issues started to manifest at school, and it frustrated me. I told him I didn't appreciate him sending me angry letters. I told him I wouldn't be his friend anymore if he was going to behave like this. His anger issues continued, and soon he punched a kid who fouled him at a church basketball game. I was so upset by that behavior, and my disappointment cut him.

But then he changed and became lighter; he was easier to be around. At one campout, I said to him, "Something's different about you. You seem really happy."

He said, "I am." He told me he was going up the mountain behind his dad's house that weekend to do some deep thinking about who he wanted to be and what he wanted to do. I told him I thought that was amazing.

That was the last time I saw Jay.

Two days later, I was walking down the stairs from my bedroom, and my mom said she needed to talk with me. Still in a sleepy fog, I didn't register the concern in her voice or the sadness on her face. We sat down and she told me that Jay had taken his own life.

Mom started to make phone calls, and I sat on the couch, confused and numb, unable to reconcile my last conversation with Jay with what I'd just been told.

Jay's mom specifically asked me to attend Jay's funeral. He'd left two letters behind—one for his parents and one for me—and his mom had read them both. Jay had taken his life on top of the mountain with his dad's gun. Many people contemplate their suicide beforehand, and I was convinced Jay had already made the decision the last time I'd seen him, when he seemed at peace.

But I couldn't bring myself to go to his service. I was too shaken up. I did go to their house a week later, and instantly upon walking in, I could feel the energy of loss and sadness and heaviness, like an invisible wet blanket smothering the air out of the room. Jay's mom was a beautiful woman, but now her face was puffy and her eyes were red. She looked like she'd aged 10 years in a few days.

I sat in front of her in their beautiful family room, trying to be strong. Then his mom handed me the letter Jay had written to me. It was on regular lined notebook paper, folded into a nice square with my name written in pencil on the top fold.

I read his words to me: "I'm sorry I couldn't be enough for you. I'm sorry I wasn't the person you wanted me to be . . ."

I didn't cry or express any emotion. I looked at his baby pictures on a shelf, at all the flowers that had been sent to his family, thinking about the hope and the love that was given to him. I couldn't understand why someone would take their life if they had everything. And I couldn't help but wonder if he'd still be alive if I hadn't broken up with him. I wasn't yet able to understand that somehow, somewhere, Jay was missing something within himself—a core truth of worth and worthiness—that no person would have ever been able to give him.

I folded the note back into a square and left their house. And I simply shut down. Subconsciously I decided I wouldn't allow boys to get close to me again. And I wouldn't allow myself to speak my truth, even if it was how I really felt—because doing so meant death.

Since I technically was not supposed to start dating until 16, for the rest of my middle and high school years, I didn't have any boyfriends. Somehow I felt that by not expressing any desire or interest in the opposite sex, I was being more holy—and I certainly felt that I was protecting myself and others.

Meeting My Husband

I met my husband—we'll call him Laerer—at church while I was a sophomore in college. I was sitting in the front row next to my roommates when this captivating guy got up to speak. He sounded as if he had it all figured out. He was the type of guy who did everything right within the church, and he had a great big smile. He seemed happy, so sure of his beliefs, in God, in my religion. My roommate leaned over to me and said, "Now that's a great guy. He is *prophet caliber.*" For a girl like me who wanted to be so good, so in line with "prophet material," which means a person who is higher up in the church, I was instantly smitten.

I wanted to be with someone who was prophet material. I wanted to be with someone who could take me to the kingdom of heaven. In my deluded mind, I thought that if I wasn't attracted to him sexually, then *that was holy*, and if I was sexually attracted, *that was not holy*.

I'm sure you can imagine what our honeymoon was like.

We did not even have sex our first night because I was so terrified. Thankfully, he didn't push me, partly because he was also uncomfortable. We had both been taught our whole lives that sex was bad and now suddenly we were supposed to do it. We had been told not to touch boobs, penises, crotches, or any of those parts! We had been told not to French kiss. More adventurous teens in high school always talked about going from base to base to base, but I never did. Now I felt I was being asked to go from first base to home base in one night. I told Laerer, "I feel like I missed out on all the fun bases."

We settled on trying second base, kissing and touching each other—but I never felt any desire. The first time we finally had sex, on day three or four into our marriage, it was very painful. My body was trying to tell me something, but I didn't know what—I thought something was wrong with me. I remember thinking, *I don't want to do that again*, but that's not how marriage was supposed to go.

Each time we had sex thereafter, it was painful and I, of course, blamed myself. My body was rejecting this partner and trying to tell me that I was not in full alignment with him—but instead of listening to my body's cues, I ignored them. Instead, I went to doctor after doctor looking for creams, serums, and steroids to help take away the pain of sex. The doctors were as confused as I was. I had no prior sexual trauma and nothing appeared to be wrong. I was given plenty of prescriptions, but nothing ever worked.

The cruelest part was that I felt like I'd done everything right. I had grown up in a very religious home and done everything that was expected of me. I didn't touch alcohol or cigarettes. I dressed modestly. I had saved myself for marriage. I had married a man that my family and community approved of. I was checking off all the boxes I knew existed:

1. Be a good girl and get good grades.

2. Go to college and get good grades.

3. Marry the perfect guy in your early 20s so you are not a misfit to society.

4. Have a child within two years of marriage.

5. Be a devoted, loving, cook-meals-on-time wife.

6. Go grocery shopping and ensure your fridge is filled and that your carpet has vacuum lines in it when your husband gets home.

7. Look like a sexy, put-together, clean, organized, stay-at-home wife. No sweats, no bun head.

The truth is that when our biggest fears and our deepest truths are about to be exposed, we do everything we can to cover them up. Part of me was questioning everything within the church, so I shoved it down by being the *best*—following all the rules and being the holiest. I was hiding *me*, and it was starting to unravel. My husband was a nice guy and a good friend, but I wanted more than that, even though I had no idea how to articulate it. My soul wanted passion, deep growth, and deep trust, and to step fully into my potential on all levels.

THE SOUL'S NUDGINGS

We all have stories we tell ourselves that keep us from leading fuller, freer, more connected lives. I told myself I was trapped by my circumstances, that I had done everything "right," that the life I'd ended up with was one I had to learn to live with, no matter how unhappy it made me. But these were not truths; they were stories, illusions, and lies.

Have you ever lied and told the same lie over and over again so often that you started believing it? If you have, you know you have to dig deep to remember that you actually made that story up. We lie to feel accepted, to have a sense of belonging and love—and more than that, to avoid the pain. That pain was my soul nudging me, screaming at me that this was not the life I was meant to live.

We all have soul nudgings. They might feel like a fluttering in your chest or stomach, or you might hear a voice or see signs in nature. Sometimes it's more of a deep knowing that you can't quite understand or explain. Maybe they come to you in yearnings of joy. It doesn't matter how our soul talks—what's important is that we remember that it *is always talking to us.* If you listen, you'll get hints about the experience that your soul wants you to live out on this earth.

Our number-one job is to honor the role our soul wants us to take on in this lifetime—but there isn't a guide or a cheat sheet to show us how it's done. No one else has ever lived your soul's life in your body. It is your task and yours alone to discover your specific purpose on earth.

If you are not listening to your inner voice but are instead listening to the noise of the world (which comes in many, many different forms, such as TV, social media, social functions, friends, and family), then you are always living someone else's truth. We are all programmed from early childhood to behave, believe, and see the world in a specific way. It is our job to tap in, to unravel that programming, and to ask ourselves, what do we really believe? What is in alignment with our soul? If you're not living your own truth, you are always living out of alignment of your soul's purpose. This lack of alignment can manifest in making you sick, making you feel anger, or simply making you feel really unhappy.

At some point, we all have to accept that our bodies, our hearts, and our minds have been trying to get our attention all along. We are all divine creatures in tune with a Universe that has our backs. The fact that we are all born at a certain time, to certain people, at a certain location, with certain genetic predispositions, is utterly amazing. In fact, according to science, there's a one in six trillion chance of each human's birth even *occurring*. From conception to first breath, there are so many obstacles and odds stacked against us that it's a statistical miracle that you and I are even alive.

I have come a long way since that day of feeling trapped in my own glass box, in my junky car, screaming out to the heavens when I didn't know what else to do. This is the story of how I came to admit to myself that the life I was living wasn't the one I was meant for. In the end, I shed old ways of thinking and being that were holding me back and learned new ways that allowed me to expand beyond what I ever thought possible.

Acting upon those truths is never easy—not at first, particularly when you're surrounded by family and friends who don't know or understand that lack of alignment you feel. That is the work of a warrior—stepping in to your truth when others have helped construct your truth into something entirely different.

When I look at my past, with its threads of life and death, miracles and despair, I have to acknowledge that tragedies and miracles happen every day all around us. Despair and joy happen at the same time, and that intertwined thread is what makes life painful and beautiful, messy and calm. You can be dancing on the biggest adrenaline high of your life and then drowning with despair in the next moment.

For those of us who are extreme planners, the unfortunate thing is that we can't always control what happens to us. Although we undoubtedly get hints and nudges from time to time, we can't predict the future. So what are we to do with this mortal body and divine soul when faced with unpleasant situations and downright tragic events?

We stand. We scream, we cry, we pray, we fall, we do whatever the heck we need to do to get through it. To make peace with it.

How? Start by recognizing the stories, the lies you have been telling yourself. For example: I am not powerful. I am not worthy of greatness. I am not beautiful. I am not worthy of love. Replace those statements with the opposite—that is your soul's truth. *I am beautiful. I am made by a loving Creator. I am powerful.*

Move with that truth! Get out there and walk, run, hike, bike, and use your body to declare your truths over and over again, physically and out loud.

Slowly, we find our feet. We find our voice. We adjust our sights. And then we Rise.

Where in your life is your body trying to talk to you through pain or discomfort?

What stories and lies have you been telling yourself and others to cover up your truth?

What is your soul trying to tell you about your life right now?

CHAPTER 2

Gifts Wrapped in Sandpaper

*For a seed to achieve its greatest expression,
it must come completely undone.
The shell cracks, its insides come out
and everything changes.
To someone who doesn't understand growth,
it would look like complete destruction.*

— CYNTHIA OCCELLI

Transformation has no timeline. It never looks like meditation, flowers, unicorns, and such. Instead, it often looks like a glimpse of heaven and feels like hell.

Two years after that day in the car, my glimpse of heaven came in the form of a wave of nausea coming over me. I had to hold on to the bathroom counter to brace myself. It didn't feel like I had the common flu symptoms, and I was late having my period. *Could it be? Could I possibly be pregnant?*

As I was waiting for my results after peeing on the pregnancy stick, I flashed back to those commercials—you know the ones—with a very attractive woman holding the stick, seeing the positive sign, and celebrating with her partner. The joy, the hope. Would I feel this hope? Ever since I could remember, I had wanted to be a mom. It felt like a rite of passage, the *next step.* I held the test stick, watching for every darkening shade as the positive signal told me, moment by moment, that I was going to be a mom.

I was thrilled, but within seconds, the fear crept in. *Was I equipped to be a mother? Would my body be able to handle it?* Over the next eight months, I found myself in new territory, with demands being placed on my body that, to be honest, wasn't handling them very well. I was extremely sick with hyperemesis gravidarum, which essentially means I threw up *everything* for my entire pregnancy—and I never really knew why.

But my daughter was healthy, and that was all that mattered to me. The world was turning just the right angle for this new beautiful arrival, and Sarah was born. She was the one thing Laerer and I had done right, and I was so thankful to be her mother. She was perfect, with beautiful blue eyes, olive skin, and a happy disposition. Our whole world revolved around her. And because our focus was entirely on her, most of my anxieties around our marriage dissipated.

My first year of motherhood was complete bliss. Laerer was a great father and a fun partner. When we put Sarah down for naps, instead of being glad to have quiet time to ourselves, we'd count the minutes until she woke up so we could hold her and play with her again. When she cried, Laerer and I would race each other, playfully pushing each other against the walls to be the first to reach her crib.

When Sarah needed middle-of-the-night diaper changes, I'd sing to her and rock her, never annoyed that I was missing out on sleep. I was so caught up in being a mother that all the doubts I had about life, love, and what I really wanted just went away—at least for that first year.

But once Sarah began to be more independent, the heaviness set in again. The bills started to pile up . . . Actually, they had never really stopped; I had just stopped paying attention. Laerer had lost job after job since we were married, mostly with no explanation—or at least, I never got one. Now that Sarah no longer absorbed *all* my attention, I finally started to see a pattern and I started questioning his truth. I no longer felt safe in the relationship, and I felt as though I was doing all the work—I was taking care of our daughter, the house, the meals, and working full-time as a fitness trainer. I was exhausted by it all and felt ill.

And then, when Sarah was five years old, I learned I was pregnant. Again. With as little intimacy as Laerer and I had, it was totally unexpected but at least explained some of the sickness and lethargy I was feeling.

I went into survival mode. I felt like all I could do was pretend everything was okay, or at least that it was going to be. *Maybe everything would get better with this second child. Maybe Laerer would find a good job and keep it. Maybe I wouldn't be so sick with this pregnancy like I was with Sarah.*

Or maybe not.

I had hyperemesis gravidarum again. I was throwing up sometimes seven times a day. As a high-risk pregnancy, I had to get frequent IVs to rehydrate, and I was put on Zofran, a medicine given to cancer patients to keep them from throwing up. My baby was quite calm despite my sickness. When I was pregnant with Sarah, she moved around all the time—she was a regular gymnast in there. This baby was content to just sit and chill.

With each checkup, I looked forward to seeing how he'd grown. He was bigger than Sarah, so I thought he might be like a gentle giant, really kind and sweet, wanting to be cuddled and held. Even before I met him, I saw his kindness and his softness.

THE VOICE INSIDE

It's said that a woman's intuition is always right. An innate gift from our Creator, our body and mind have the uncanny ability to sense the truth of the matter— sometimes wrapped in a tiny feeling of unease in the air or signaled by the prickle of energy and excitement.

Our advanced auditory receptors can detect a slightly unnatural or forced tone in someone's voice, letting us know they're lying or withholding information. With one glance at a lover's face, in milliseconds we feel in the pit of our stomachs that there's been a grave indiscretion. In better moments, like just before our best friend calls us to catch up, her name and image pop into our mind and our smile barely has the chance to form before we're picking up the phone to accept her call. "I was just thinking about you!" we say in awe. We don't even notice we have this gift, but we use it every day, every moment.

Even though we each have this intuition, we also have the ability to choose to listen—or not—when our Spidey senses kick in. Some women are taught to embrace it from a young age; the more they listen, the more they are able to grow as they tune in to the world inside and around themselves. Others, whether under the cloud of disbelieving or discouraging parents, painful circumstances, or strict religion, learn early on to ignore the whisper within, stuffing it down until there's hardly a memory of an inner voice at all.

But you can only forget for so long.

One afternoon, when I was seven months pregnant, the house was surprisingly quiet. Sarah was out with her father running errands after lunch, giving me a rare moment of stillness and peace as I sat in the rocking chair in front of the big bay window that overlooked the front yard and tree-lined street.

The rocking chair had a special place in my heart because it had been in my husband's family for years, passed down from generation to generation. Because there wasn't any padding on the seat, it wasn't really comfortable, but I loved it anyway. I'd fed and rocked Sarah to sleep many nights in this chair, with this same view. Soon I'd be rocking my second child to sleep in my arms, in the same chair where generations of women had rocked their babies.

Without thinking, I placed my hands on my belly. It had become the natural resting place these last few weeks to feel my baby move throughout the day.

Because I gained so little weight due to my hyperemesis gravidarum, I could see different definitions of an elbow or a back rolling through my belly. It was always fun for me, especially at night, to watch the show. It was now around 3 P.M., a time when he was usually quite active. I thought he might still be asleep so I began rubbing and pushing my belly gently—I wanted to wake him up and enjoy these moments of alone time with him! For months I had been dreaming about him. *What is this little boy going to be like? Who is he going to look like? Would he love sports like me or have musical talent and decide to play the violin? Would he and Sarah have an instant bond?*

He still wasn't waking up, so I started talking to him. I was in such a happy space, feeling excitement and joy, but then a flash in my mind jolted me: *Something is not right.*

I tensed my back slightly and held my belly tighter as I sat straight in the chair.

Instantly there was another voice. It was almost like the familiar cartoon scene of one voice on one shoulder and another voice on the other shoulder.

As soon as the first voice said, "Something is not right," the other snapped back, "Stop being paranoid."

The first voice said, "Even if he was sleeping, you would have probably woken him up with those nudges and he would have kicked at least once."

The other voice said, "You are so paranoid all the time! He is fine. He was kicking this morning, remember?"

Although the truest and deepest part of me wanted to listen and take action in some way, the part of me that had been running the show for most of my life—the perfect do-gooder who did everything that was expected of her—was stronger.

I had learned to shove down my true voice my whole life. And now it was tapping on my shoulder, gently calling attention to all the areas of my life where I'd done the "right" thing instead of listening to my soul.

Is this really where you want to go to school?

Are you made for this life you've chosen?

Is this the kind of relationship you want?

Is this the home you want to live in?

Is this what you want to believe in?

If I listened now—married with a second baby on the way and doing everything I was supposed to be doing—then what? Listening to my own truth would mean *everything would change.*

But in the stillness of the room, the voice said again, "Listen to me. Something is not right."

If we're lucky, the reintroduction to the deepest part of ourselves shows up like a sweet spring rain, gently awakening our senses to the beauty around us and inviting us to come out and play. But other times it's more like a tsunami, where emotions rise without warning and crash over us, the pressure holding us inches below the surface of sanity.

I ignored my personal tsunami. I got up from the rocking chair and busied myself with doing the dishes.

ANGELS AMONG US

I had been seeing a doctor every week for ultrasounds and to monitor my health; they were always checking on my baby and always checking on me. On the day of my next scheduled checkup, I began to bleed. Then I started having contractions, so we all jumped in the car and headed to the hospital a few hours before my appointment.

As soon as we got to the hospital, things went into overdrive. Nurses rushed to get me in a wheelchair and pushed me into a delivery room. There were a lot of lights and bodies swirling around me, an orchestra of organized chaos. We had just enough time to call our parents, which sent both sets into a sprint to get to us, my parents catching the next flight down and Laerer's parents making the two-hour drive up.

The doctor hurried into the room soon after and hooked me to an ultrasound machine.

They couldn't find a heartbeat—the silence that is every mother's worst nightmare. The clinician said,

"There's something wrong. We don't know what's going on. We need to hurry and induce you."

Sarah was in the room with us when we were told that no heartbeat could be detected. But there was no time to explain the details, no time to answer any questions she might have had or to comfort her heart at the thought of losing her baby brother. The staff quickly moved Sarah out of the room and into the hallway where my in-laws were now waiting, and I was moved to a different room to prepare for labor.

I flashed back to just a few days earlier when I was sitting in the rocking chair and didn't feel him move, and I began to wonder if he'd passed away on that same day. *But maybe he's still alive*, I thought. The medical team was rushing around, far too busy trying to save my son to have time to explain everything to me.

And yet, even in the midst of that panic, as I was being prepped for delivery, a sense of peace came over me. I said a prayer and asked for everything to turn out the way it was supposed to turn out. But I wasn't praying for him to make it. I was praying for Laerer and me to be strong, and for the divine outcome to happen.

That prayer shocked me, even as I thought it. I was very aware that I wasn't asking for what my conscious brain would normally say. But when you're in a state of deep prayer, the truth comes out. I said what my soul wanted to say: "Please help me to accept whatever will come. Please help us to be strong for whatever comes. Please watch over Sarah."

I became hyperaware of my body and my surroundings. I could see and hear the doctor and nurses working on me, and the epidural was so strong, I didn't feel any pain. I could feel the pressure of my body being moved around. I focused on the stark white walls of the hospital room and the beeping sounds from the machines.

Nobody was really telling me what was going on, but my soul knew. My little boy was not going to make it.

The drugs were keeping me calm, but I was also in shock, mentally and emotionally. I wasn't hysterical or sleeping or talking. I was just lying there. Waiting. Pushing.

Someone said, "He is coming." As a preemie, he was little, so there were no issues with a vaginal birth, no risk of me tearing during delivery. He came right out, and as soon as he emerged, the energy in the room shifted. I looked over at Laerer to see if I was hallucinating or dreaming because I felt I'd entered into another realm, which felt like heaven.

We were no longer in a sterile, white hospital room with beeping machines. A force field of serenity surrounded us, as the nurses, now glowing in white, rushed the baby out.

Laerer and I waited and waited, growing anxious and wanting to see our son. Finally, after what seemed like hours, the nurses walked back into the room, gliding with that peaceful movement you get from the most loving, mindful grandma who loves you unconditionally . . . but my son was nowhere to be seen.

I searched the nurses' faces, hoping for an easy explanation. But they looked different and they felt different, like they had transformed into angels, a heavenly glow surrounding each of them. The nurses stood around us, surrounding us with pure love as the doctor walked in. I had been meeting with this man every week. If this rigid analytical doctor also looked angelic, then I knew I wasn't hallucinating. I knew I was experiencing something just for me. Something to let me know that despite what was being taken from me, I was supported and loved.

The doctor placed his hands gently on my shoulder. "Your son is not here. He has passed on. We don't know what caused his death, but we will look into it. Would you like to see him and hold him?"

As soon as the doctor asked the question, I had a deep knowing—a message imparted to me from somewhere else—that everything was okay. Not that it was *going to be* okay, but that it already was. This was how it was supposed to be. It felt like I had already lived this loss. I had already seen all of this. I had already felt all of this. It was like I had already known my son wasn't going to live.

"Yes," I said.

Moments later, nurses brought him to me, and again, there was such a sense of peace. He had a little hat on and was wrapped so tenderly in a little blanket. They were gentle with him as they placed him in my arms. I was thankful that angels were holding my baby, and I felt like I was surrounded by my ancestors.

Although my tears were rolling freely down my face, I wasn't hysterical or sobbing. I was holding my beautiful son in the bed while Laerer stood over my shoulder. Laerer was crying, too, but not sobbing hard. We were admiring our creation, our little boy. The boy whose room was ready and waiting, filled with tiny clothes he would never wear.

He looked a lot like my husband and a lot like the little boy that I had seen in my dreams. He was so tiny, with soft skin, perfect lips, and his father's nose. I decided to name him Hap, after my great-grandpa. I had never met him, but everyone always talked about him being the most kind, happy guy, and really athletic. They called him "Hap" for short because he was always happy. And even though we hadn't been alive at the same time, I remember feeling his presence there, along with an overwhelming energy and love.

I told Laerer that our son's name was Hap and he was going to be just fine, that everyone was going to take care of him. I talked to my great-grandpa Hap, as if he were right next to me in the room, telling him thanks for taking care of our son and loving him.

I held my baby for many, many hours. So long, in fact, that the nurses were trying to figure out how to get him out of my arms. Every hour or so, they kept checking on me. I'm sure it was awkward for them, as they tried to honor the process.

Eventually the nurses came back in the room and gently said they needed to take my son. That was really, really hard. I didn't want them to take him. I wanted to hold him forever.

I felt like a piece of me was being ripped away—my very own creation from my very own blood, sweat, and tears. I felt a physical longing in my arms to hold him forever. I felt the heaviness in my heart of knowing that I would not get to see him grow to be a toddler, running around the home with a bare bum. I wouldn't get to see him giggle or witness his sister hugging him.

My heart hurt, especially for Sarah. She was the one who talked to him through my belly every night. Telling him all her jokes and all her plans for them together. She would read to him, sing to him, and was so excited to have a little brother that she would get to show off to all her friends.

We finally said our good-byes to him. It felt like a collective mission and a collective energy of sharing all our prayers and love with him. It was a painful moment of reality to physically release my son from my arms and from my body, as he left the room, never to return.

Wearing a Mask

On the day we took Sarah home from the hospital after she was born, all snug and tight in her car seat, we drove so slowly, obeying every traffic light and stop sign, checking each direction twice at the intersections.

On this trip home, Laerer drove like that again, even though the car seat was empty. He drove so slowly, not because there was any reason to be cautious but because we were going home to broken dreams. I was going home to a room full of adorable baby clothes, a built crib, and all the scents of baby lotion and baby powder, but I had nothing to show for it.

As is typical when tragedy hits a small community, everybody was at our house when we got home. Both Laerer's mom and my mom thought it was a good idea to make a big dinner, so I walked in to see the table all set for a feast. No one was celebrating, of course, but everyone was talking.

I was trying to be a *good girl*—even when I'd just lost my son. I should have given myself permission to be sad and go in my room and curl up on my bed with my covers to shut out reality. Instead, I felt compelled to take care of people who had come to my small home without my invitation.

While I was thankful for all the food and the support, there was a lot of small, stupid talk, and I just sat there pretending I was fine. No one asked any questions, or even really talked about it. You could hear the clanging of plates and forks and gulps of water as much as the thick fog of sadness that no one wanted to admit was there.

It wasn't just me—we *all* wanted to curl up and cry— but none of us allowed ourselves to.

My mom stayed with us for about a week in the guest room because even though I didn't have a newborn to care for, I had still just had a baby and it was hard to move around. And as much as my heart was breaking, I knew hers was as well. Every night, the sadness would hit me in heavy waves and I would howl and moan into my bedsheets. I thought nobody could hear me, but my mother could. So could Sarah. I would cry, and Laerer would cry next to me. Most nights I'd cry myself to sleep and the mornings always came too soon.

My body was showing all the signs of having had a baby. My chest was full of milk, but because I couldn't release the milk, I got mastitis and a fever, and my chest hurt so badly. I'd been advised not to pump, because the more you pump, the more milk your body produces. Instead, I was supposed to stand in hot showers and let it leak out of my body, onto the shower floor, and down the drain.

Every cell in my body wanted to feed a baby—and I couldn't do anything about it. I stood there several times a day in my hot shower like a crack addict without a hit. My body was begging me, "I want that baby now! I am craving holding a baby!" I still had a belly, my breasts were full, and my arms were empty.

I found myself going into a very deep, dark depression. This once excited, exuberant, outgoing, fit, athletic woman didn't leave her home for three months. I wouldn't even go out to buy essentials for my daughter. I felt like I didn't know who I was, other than a ghost in this lifetime.

On the day of Hap's funeral, we released hundreds of blue balloons into the sky. It felt fitting. It gave us all something to do, let us be in our own thoughts and emotions, and allowed us to send those thoughts and prayers up into the sky.

Sarah, who was processing Hap's death in her own way, chose to release a balloon. My daughter was young, just five years old, but she knew what was going on. Although she was at the hospital during those two days, I hadn't allowed her to hold Hap or even see him because I thought it might be too traumatic, that maybe she wouldn't understand.

But perhaps that wasn't the right call. Days after the funeral, Sarah was still upset that I didn't let her hold him. She said, "I never got to see him. I wanted to see him. I wanted to say good-bye. I wanted to hold him and you didn't let me." She couldn't understand why we held that away from her, even though I tried to explain that I didn't want to make her sad or scared.

Like the rest of us, Sarah would cry sometimes. For months afterward, we would hear her talking in the middle of the night, and it was at such a normal level of conversation that I would wake up confused. After looking at the clock and confirming that it was still the middle of the night, I would walk down the hall and peek in the door, and she would be sitting up on her bed as if she were talking to someone.

A friend had given us a statue of Jesus with a little boy sitting on his lap, and she'd put that statue by her bed—that's who she was talking to, as if the statue were Hap. She would draw picture after picture after picture for him during the daytime.

I told Sarah that I heard her talking at night.

And she said, "I am talking to Hap."

Intrigued and a little worried, I responded, "Okay. What is Hap saying?"

Without missing a beat, she said, "Oh, we are just talking about different things. I am showing him my pictures."

Part of me wondered if she was making this up, but at the same time, *I knew she wasn't.*

We eventually heard the results of the autopsy, such as they were. I had one of the best doctors in Utah for high-risk pregnancies and even he was dumbfounded. Initially he thought that maybe the nurses had done something or the baby had gotten an infection, but the results of the autopsy were clear—there was nothing. They couldn't find anything wrong, no reason why my son died. To this day, they still don't know what happened.

The week after his passing, I received a card in the mail—a picture of Christ holding a little boy's hand walking through a forest. The moment I opened the card and saw the picture I broke down crying, because the little boy had brown hair and brown eyes, and was wearing a red shirt and little blue pants. *That's exactly what I thought he would look like.* It felt like a gentle reminder that Hap was still there, somewhere, whole and free, even if I couldn't see him or talk with him like Sarah could.

Death stirs up such a whirlwind of emotions. In the hospital room holding my beautiful son, I had experienced such a calm place of knowing, even though there was chaos happening all around me. But it didn't last, and soon after, the extreme depression took over. A belief of worthlessness seeped into every bone in my body. I could pretend to be okay during the day when there were a million things to do. But at night, when I was alone in the dark with my thoughts, I started to think about how nice it would be to never have to think or feel anything again.

Darkest before the Dawn

The tile floor was cool under my feet as I leaned against the kitchen counter. I had made my way through the dark, creeping from my bed to the small kitchen—the room that contained the only destructive weapons in our home. Knives . . . knives could cut the pain out of my body. I could end it here and now. It would be better for everyone this way.

There was no noise anywhere. Both my daughter and my husband were sleeping peacefully in their beds.

The ache that had been consuming me piece by piece since I had watched the nurses walk away with my baby had nearly taken me over. I felt like I couldn't breathe. The tightness around my chest and neck felt like a snake wrapping its evil, ropy body around me, cinching in tighter with each raspy breath I took. I didn't want to *die*, necessarily. I just didn't want to *live* anymore.

It had been several weeks since we had buried Hap. I had tried so hard to be strong, to be fine, to continue being a mother and a wife. I had mastered the fake smile. I'd repeated the lines "I am fine" and "We are all getting through one day at a time" so often that I didn't even think about the words anymore as they tumbled from my mouth.

It was so much easier to lie about what I was really feeling because if I let out a small trickle of truth, my whole world would implode. Truth would spew like projectile vomit all over my family, my husband, my neighbors, my child, and myself. And like all moms, I didn't want any of my truth-telling to affect my child. I wanted our lives to look neat and clean, full of strength, full of hope. *Full of bullshit*. The truth was, I didn't have the courage to tell someone, "I'm not okay."

I doubt I was fooling anyone with my make-believe game face; I certainly wasn't fooling myself. Several people *had* reached out and offered to help in various ways, but what could they do? No one knew the depth of the pain I was in. I didn't know anyone who had lost a child. I felt completely alone.

I crawled on my knees to the small drawer in the corner that held the *sharp* knives, the ones that were rarely used. There were no pills or alcohol in the home to drown myself in, and certainly no guns, even though I grew up on a farm. *I hated guns.* Guns killed innocent animals and a gun had killed my 12-year-old boyfriend.

A vision of Jay flashed through my mind. I saw his brown hair and big smile. He cared about me. He wanted me to like him for him. He loved deeply, and one day, somehow the pain was too much. I now understood exactly what he was feeling. He was sick of saying, "I am fine." He was tired. He felt alone. He felt completely misunderstood. He felt like a fraud.

What about his mom? Why did he do this to all of us? Why didn't we see the signs?

But we did see the signs. We just didn't know what we were seeing and didn't know what to do. He was withdrawn. He had started to isolate himself. He had asked to be loved. And I had said no.

I hadn't gone to his funeral because I was too overwhelmed with emotions I couldn't even describe. Now here I was thinking about my family at my funeral. They would be so mad at me, like I was mad at Jay. How dare he be so selfish. *How dare I be so selfish.*

I sat there on the cold floor holding the knife, in my safe home with my little girl and husband sleeping down the hall.

My father and I had installed this tile floor together. We were on a shoestring budget, and the kitchen had needed a serious renovation. My dad had volunteered to drive from Montana to Utah to help me save a few thousand dollars in labor costs and to teach me how to lay tile with him.

That was his love language, acts of service. He wanted to show me he cared. When I was in high school, he'd start my car in the mornings so it would warm up, and scrape the snowfall from the windows when it was zero degrees outside. While he wasn't one for hugs or saying, "I love you," he showed his feelings the only way he knew how, through hard work.

We had spent a few long days laying this two-toned tile, and I loved it. Could I take my life on this tile and spill my blood everywhere? That felt so disrespectful. My mind went from rational thought to despair within seconds, my emotions flip-flopping with each breath.

"You are such an exaggerator. If you really meant it, you would kill yourself when no one was around," one voice said.

"I hate myself. I am a terrible mom. Please, pain, stop!" the other cried.

"You are just trying to get attention. You've seen these stories before. They slit their wrists because it takes too long to die and someone finds them and rescues them. You *want* to be rescued."

Did I?

I knew what had to be done to end my pain. I felt I didn't deserve to be alive. As the floor began to puddle with my tears, I could feel my throat opening up, wanting to breathe, but instead of breaths, uncontrollable, unrecognizable sounds came out. I was sobbing, gasping, groaning. I was desperate for a lot of things. Desperate to feel. To feel in control. To feel vibrant. To feel happy. To feel worthy.

No. You are not worthy.

As I ran the knife across my wrists, the pain on my skin felt lighter than the pain in my heart, but it was not very effective. *Damn, I don't even have enough money to buy decent knives! These are so cheap, they barely cut tomatoes, and they are doing a terrible job on my wrists.*

I was making small slicing marks in my flesh, but if I was going to be successful with this crappy knife, I'd have to wield it like a saw. My sobs got louder, and my husband woke up. He found me and crouched down next to me, shocked and hurt by what he saw, putting his arms around me.

There's something about when someone arrives in the midst of your despair that makes you feel like you are even more pathetic, and you start to spiral out of control. I started crying louder, filling up the kitchen with my groans.

Amazingly, Laerer remained calm, like he'd been trained to rescue a suicide victim. Perhaps he didn't believe that I was serious, although I know he believed my suffering, as he'd been feeling it, too. There, on the kitchen floor, he started talking me down from the ledge. Reminding me of my truth: I am a mom; I am needed; I am loved. Pain doesn't last forever. I am not alone.

I made him promise to not ever tell anyone what happened that night. And I decided that I'd give life a second chance.

WE ARE NEVER BROKEN

Despite that moment of peace in the hospital, I collapsed when I got home. I believe my spirit knew more than my consciousness, and it took a while before my consciousness could rise up to meet the part of me that already understood.

My grandfather used to say, "Good things happen to good people." The idea resonated so strongly with me that I once wrote a high school paper on the subject. But then when difficult and painful things happened in my life, I didn't know how to take them. If bad things happened to me, did that mean I was bad?

I struggled to reconcile these ideas in my mind for a long time. I eventually came to understand that enlightenment is not an endgame—once you have it, that doesn't mean you have it forever. Life is like that. It's not a straight line. It ebbs and flows.

This experience brought me to my knees, but it taught me that just because something feels incredibly painful doesn't mean it isn't affecting your spirit in a profound and positive way. It taught me to fight for my truth, no matter what.

In the great search for truth, there are many lies we have to shed. One of those lies is, "I am broken." I hear this a lot in my work with women. Teachers and gurus trying to connect with people who have been badly hurt or who are depressed will sometimes say, "You are broken. We are going to fix your broken heart. We are going to fix your broken soul."

In reality, nothing is ever *broken*. Energy is never *stopped*. There is no such thing as stuck energy or *stuck anything*. This is an illusion. Life is a never-ending cycle.

Energy is always moving and flowing—always—including in our lives. You are never stuck emotionally, spiritually, or physically. Even if you feel stagnant, you are always moving because you are always breathing and capable of a new thought and a new direction. You could be moving in a direction you don't want to be moving, or you could be moving very, very slowly, but there is always movement.

All the tools we need are within us. Our spiritual journey is about uncovering and connecting with that which is already there rather than seeking out something we need or lack. Whether you call this force God, Source, or the Universe, I believe it's the same for all of us. The Universe provides us with what we need, even when we can't fully understand or accept the gifts.

MY UNFORESEEN GIFTS

For reasons I may never understand, Hap was never meant to inhabit this world by my side. I call Hap's passing a "gift wrapped in sandpaper." Gifts don't always come wrapped in pretty paper and tied with shiny bows. This was a hard lesson for me to learn.

I understand it may take time to see the gift in any trauma. But this is what I know—without pain, we cannot learn what we are truly made of. Without learning pain on a cellular level, we cannot truly empathize with others in their pain. Pain is our gift. Pain is where true character is revealed.

And through the deep pain of losing Hap, I gained three gifts I will forever be grateful for.

The First Gift

My first gift from Hap was empathy. Deep loss has made me more empathetic and more able to relate to other humans and to other conditions in life. When others share their losses with me, I can relate and better understand how to serve them. The death of my son taught me the powerful lessons of compassion, empathy, and nonjudgment. I realized that we are *all* fighting some sort of battle that others know nothing about. We all experience suffering on some level. Everyone processes trauma and grief in their own way. So instead of judging others when I find myself annoyed at something they do or say, I now respond with kindness, knowing that they, too, must be suffering in some way.

There is no right way, and there is no wrong way to process pain. There is only *the* way. *Your* way. And that way is perfect. It is a part of your unraveling, a part of your journey. It may not look like anyone else's and that is okay. Some may judge the way I handled the death of my son, but the truth is, you don't know how you will react or respond to anything in life until it happens to you. I have compassion and deep respect for others on their journey, knowing that each action and reaction is a part of their story.

The Second Gift

The second gift was that Hap woke me up to my voice, my truth. It seems a little ironic that it took me trying to wake *him* up that day in the rocking chair to start such a chain reaction, but that's what happened. Even though I wasn't able to save his life, he saved mine. His death brought me to a place where I didn't care about anything—and I needed to let go of so many of the things I cared about to make room for what I *really* loved and valued and felt was true.

Before Hap's death, I had been putting on a mask, lying to myself and everyone around me. I was questioning my beliefs in my religion, but instead of stepping in and looking at them, I would pretend to be the most faithful.

And I did the same thing with my marriage. I was not really happy with Laerer and didn't feel physically drawn to him. But instead of acknowledging that, I would talk him up to every person I would meet, because I was trying to *convince myself.* When you feel as though you have to maintain a façade to please others, you become a masterful liar. We tell ourselves lies all the time to make ourselves feel better about the conditions we are not willing to leave.

When Hap died, I didn't care about any of that anymore. I didn't care what anyone thought.

For those first three months after Hap's death, I hid from the world and I hid from myself. But as I slowly started to heal, I began to reconnect with others and, most important, with myself. And with time, I found the courage to start sharing my story. As painful as it was—and still is—Hap's passing was the beginning of my awakening. It was the beginning of using my voice, though I couldn't even talk about it for a year. It terrified me at first, but I found that the more I talked about it, the more I healed. And the more I connected with others, the less pain I felt inside my soul. I told this story again and again and again before I could tell it without crying . . . until one day, it became empowering. I was empowered by my own story, as I realized that this moment of despair was when I started to get my own wings and listen to my own soul.

The biggest revelation I had was that so many others had also experienced the pain of losing a child. I believe this happened for me so I could live out the life I'm living today.

The great unraveling will bring you to your knees and make you curl up in a ball in your bed sometimes. That's okay. That's part of the shedding and transformation. The old must become new again.

Radical truth-telling allows us to use our voices and share our truths, our stories, so we can heal as a collective. So we can heal the pain that we are shoving down. So we can ultimately show up in our power, love, and grace and heal the world.

The Third Gift

My third gift was that Hap saved my life. He saved my life through teaching me how to truly *live*. Without the pain of Hap's death, I wouldn't know bliss and I wouldn't know how to truly live. And without the fall, I wouldn't have been able to Rise. Without the fall, I would have continued sleepwalking through a life that was not mine. A life that left me uninspired, unfulfilled, and mediocre. Hap's death brought me back to life, and for that, I will always be grateful.

Being at rock bottom woke me up to life. To extreme pain. Extreme joy. To myself. It dismantled all my previous paradigms. It disrupted the life I was living on autopilot and forced me to take back the wheel. Once my soul healed, I was able to see the beauty that came from the pain. The gift of the struggle.

The Universe is always speaking to us, constantly placing things in our path that force us to grow. Sometimes she leaves little pebbles on the road that may cause discomfort on our bare feet. And other times she hurls boulders our way, which cause the deepest pain in our hearts. Losing my son was one of these boulders.

Every experience holds within it a lesson that contributes to our growth. And often, the most turbulent times that send us on a spiral straight to rock bottom are the ones that teach us the greatest lessons.

When you're in the thick of it, it's hard to see the lesson. But once our hearts have healed and the fog in our minds has slowly evaporated, we can gain the most beautiful sense of clarity. And that boulder that was thrown at us begins to look like the brightest diamond, casting a light on our souls.

What do you feel were the hidden gifts of your darkest hour?

What do you feel you were meant to learn through your pain?

How can you reframe your experience, to find the lesson?

CHAPTER 3

Small Hinges Move Big Doors

We delight in the beauty of the butterfly,
but rarely admit the changes it has gone
through to achieve that beauty.

— MAYA ANGELOU

I spent the first three months after Hap's birth primarily in bed. A normal day for me started with my daughter coming in the room, saying she was hungry (which, like most kids, was *always*) and me trying to quickly strategize ways to get her fed without having to move. "Can you find something to eat?" became the norm. She would figure it out and move chairs over to the counter to climb up and get her own food in the kitchen, because that is the spirit she is.

The house was so messy, and I am such a clean freak, but it didn't even matter to me. I did manage to get out of bed to use the bathroom and to shower, so that was *something*. When you lose something and go through depression, there is a point when you start not to care.

You start to get real with yourself and say, "Whatever, I give up. Screw it. I surrender."

Most days, Sarah wanted to go outside and play, and I knew I should go with her, but I refused. Instead, I would tell her to go outside and would try to explain where the end of the sidewalk was, because I didn't want her to go into the busy road.

I couldn't leave the house. I was terrified I might run into somebody I knew who hadn't heard what had happened and would ask where the baby was. I did not want to see or talk to anyone, so I didn't even go to the grocery store for about three months. Instead, Laerer would pick up the staples and make dinner.

A few times during those months, I grabbed my shoes, pumping myself up to take the big leap and take the first step outside, but as soon as I started to wonder who I might see, I would lose momentum and climb back into bed. Every single day, I told myself, *You need to go outside.* Gradually I would walk to the mailbox and back, and those were huge victories. My goal was to walk around the block, where people could actually see me.

The truth is that while I don't believe anyone is ever *broken*, I sure felt that way. I felt like a shell of a human. I was going through the motions, but not fully awake. Not *feeling*, for fear it would be too much to handle. My soul was still talking to me in so many ways, but I was completely ignoring those messages. And that, of course, couldn't last. My body wouldn't let me get away with it— it was going to *force* me to listen. Our bodies are much smarter than we give them credit for.

My body was *insisting* that I get out of bed and just *move*. I felt this deep knowing that I would feel better if I got out of bed, into fresh air, and walked. Deep down I was starting to feel restless.

It wasn't like one day I woke up and said to myself, "I'm going to be my biggest rescuer." But little by little, as I started to listen to what my body was trying to tell me, leaning on my knowledge of the power of movement, and implementing small bouts of movement, I knew it would save me and my heart would show me the way if I would just . . . let . . . go.

Sometimes we all need to curl up in a ball and take to our beds. That's okay—but we can't stay there forever. That time we spend curled up in our cocoon *is* valuable— it's a part of transformation.

NATURAL MEDICINE

While I couldn't control the events of the past, I knew I could control my own life. I couldn't change Hap's death, but there was another child who needed me . . . I needed to show up for myself so that I could be the mother I wanted to be for Sarah. And so I tried to make more of an effort to at least get up a few times a day and make breakfast or help Sarah with projects around the house. And then one day it happened: I started to lace up my shoes, even while the voice in my head was telling me to stop, to crawl back in bed. My soul was begging me to get up, to move, to be in nature. After what felt like tying the longest shoelace of my life, I finally had both shoes on.

I shuffled to the door and stepped out into the sunshine. I started my slow walk around the block. I noticed the cracks in the sidewalk, the trees lining the street. The older homes with little white picket fences around them. Taking the second turn, I felt something stir inside of me. My chest was pounding. My heart was opening. I heard the birds singing and felt the sun glistening through the leaves of the trees, my heart expanding, beating faster and faster, and my soul could not be contained another minute.

At the third turn, my soul burst open, knocking down all my pretend walls, spilling over into nature, as tears streamed down my face. I was releasing and allowing all of it to spill out of me. With each step and each tear, my heart felt lighter and lighter, as I walked around the entire block.

That may seem like such a small step forward, but it changed everything for me. It catalyzed my healing, on every level.

Movement had always been important to me—I was a trainer, after all—but my understanding of fitness was always on a physical level. With that simple act of walking around the block, my body taught me that movement could also support me mentally and emotionally.

I had heard, of course, that movement can help with depression, but being in that state myself allowed me to truly understand, on a cellular level, just what that meant. Movement is the first step we take to clean out the cobwebs of the soul, to awaken and remember our healing capabilities, our happiness, and our power.

I started to walk around the neighborhood every day and I knew on an internal level that movement would heal the deepest parts of my soul. I've never let go of movement since then—I've depended on it. I now truly understand that movement is not about counting calories or fitting into that dress; it is the most powerful tool we all have to step into our spirit.

Trusting my body in this way prompted me to explore what else I could do for it. I realized that in the months after Hap's death, I had gotten way off track with my nutrition, often not eating at all. With my newfound sense of energy and motivation from daily movement, I knew that I had to help myself along with healing foods.

I went online and to the library to research foods that could help with depression. As I researched, I became absorbed and empowered by *true nutrition.* Like so many of us, I had been completely taken in by the idea of low-fat, reduced-fat, fat-free American nutrition, but now I was learning about food as a powerful medicine.

I was particularly drawn to superfoods, those basic, ancient foods that have sustained and healed people around the world for centuries. I learned that this kind of healthy eating didn't have to come from a lot of pills, it didn't have to be woo-woo, and it certainly didn't have to be gross-tasting. Armed with curiosity and passion, I unraveled the truth about these foods, and experimented with how to bridge them from these ancient ways of life to the mainstream.

In my tiny kitchen, with my even tinier budget, I used these superfoods to create five-ingredient recipes that Sarah and I both enjoyed. I could feel the energy within my body starting to shift, to grow. The fog in my brain, that fog of grief, finally started to lift, and I felt I could truly see again. As I felt that healing in my body, I felt my attention and my enthusiasm, my passion, shift back to my work. I shared my recipes with my clients and was so gratified to see the changes they began experiencing as well.

As I began to feel better mentally and physically, I was able to see the signs that my relationship with my husband still wasn't working. Apart from the year of bliss after Sarah was born, things hadn't improved all that much since the day *five years earlier* when I lost it in the car on campus.

I kept feeling the floor continue to vanish from beneath me, as I found more and more bottoms to drop to. I was discovering lies in my relationship and lies within myself *about* my relationship. And I couldn't do it anymore.

Laerer got fired soon after our son's death. The reasons why weren't clear, but I was in too much of a haze for it to really register. I didn't ask too many questions, because I wasn't sure I wanted to hear the answers. He'd probably just use the same excuses I'd heard before: He was overqualified. His boss was a jerk. His working conditions were poor and he deserved more money.

He would always leave in the mornings and go to a job, or say he was trying to find a job. He would leave around 7 and then come back around 4 or 5 in the afternoon. I never knew where he was or what he was doing.

I think this was part of my husband's unraveling, too. There was so much chaos during this time, so many things he did that didn't make any sense. I'll never know his side of the truth, but when I realized he had lost the seventh job in two years, I began to suspect that Laerer was someone I barely knew at all.

But I still didn't listen to my soul. We grew distant, but I didn't listen to my own intuition. I didn't make a change . . . yet.

Our Miracle

Several months after Hap's funeral, Sarah told me that Hap was going to come back. The first time she said it, I dismissed it as her active imagination and desire to have a brother, although it wasn't anything I'd have expected to hear from my six-year-old. The second time she said it, I gave her the suspicious side eye. *What was she talking about? Was she saying she wanted another sibling? Did she know something I didn't?*

For months, she stuck with this story. Honestly, I was still in the process of emerging from the fog, so I didn't pay her that much attention. I thought it was her way of processing the loss. That is, until I found out I was pregnant. Again. Not just pregnant—*nearly five months pregnant.*

I'd gone to the doctor because I was feeling sick and assumed it was part of the overall depression. Maybe I'd picked up a cold or flu with such a depressed immune system and a depressed life in general. My body still showed all the signs of just having had a baby so my system was already jacked up. I hadn't even had a period yet after Hap's delivery. My relationship with my husband had been so strained that we'd only been together once since Hap's death.

Apparently, it only takes one time.

Learning I was already in the second term of an unexpected pregnancy was one thing. Being told my due date for my surprise baby girl was January 17, the exact same date as Hap's birth and death—that jolted me. I knew on a deep cellular level that her arrival in the world was no accident. She was a miracle.

So I drove home to deliver the news: We were nearly five months pregnant with baby number three, a girl who would be born on Hap's birthday. This was a huge shock to Laerer. He struggled with it, and continued to struggle with accepting her in my belly. During the first two pregnancies, he'd talk to Sarah and Hap through my tummy, placing his hands over the surface to feel them kick. With this pregnancy, he was very distant, almost as though he feared the worst might happen again. I knew he was scared of becoming attached just to have her taken away. But I knew that she was going to live. *I just knew.* The odds of her conception, the odds of her due date— it felt divine to me and I knew that once she was born, Laerer would fall madly in love with her.

Sarah, on the other hand, was ecstatic from day one! She even named her, calling her Samantha from that very first day I came home from the doctor's appointment. The name stuck!

I felt alone without Laerer's excitement, but I was determined to do everything I could to protect this baby. I'm proud to say, the next time my gut spoke to me, the next time I heard a gentle voice urging me to pay attention to my body, I listened.

TRUSTING MY INTUITION

Although I was so grateful to avoid months of extreme nausea this time around, with my history I was still considered a high-risk pregnancy. Day after day, in preparation for this new life, I continued to do "small hinge" work, by eating healing foods and moving daily, which helped me wake up and trust myself more. Part of that included following my gut and switching doctors at the last minute.

I knew that this was all perfect, that Samantha was coming as a gift. Yet appointment after appointment, I was told again and again that she was high risk. Always, something was wrong. At one appointment, I was told that she probably wasn't going to make it. The next time, I was told she could have Down syndrome. On my next visit, the nursing staff took me through the NICU to show me what could possibly happen in all different areas.

But I didn't believe any of it. I just didn't believe God would give me this child that I certainly didn't plan for, on the same date as the death of my son, just to take her away. I went through the motions of hearing the doctors tell me all the things I should be prepared for, should the worst happen again.

But then I started feeling like something was *off.* So I expressed my opinion that I felt she needed to be delivered sooner rather than later. Instead of listening to me, they offered me a *prescription.* The best doctor in the region—the same doctor who had delivered Hap—told me, "You need some Valium. You're a little paranoid because we're getting closer to her due date."

I didn't want Valium. I didn't want any medicine. I decided I needed a second opinion. Finally, I was listening to my intuition!

There are moments when you're awake. There are moments when you get ruthless with your truth. And there are moments when you get grounded. I tuned in to all those things and stood my ground. The next day I drove to see another doctor in the small town of Logan, Utah, about two hours away. I told him my entire medical history concerning my pregnancies and he ran some tests. After receiving the results, he knew that my daughter was in her final few weeks in the womb, with a healthy heartbeat. But he didn't think the baby had grown enough in these last few weeks. This is rare at the final stages, as most babies have their biggest growth in the last month.

He felt it was best to bring her into the world, even if it was a little early, versus taking our chances that something could go wrong in the next few weeks while in the womb. He based these decisions on medical knowledge as well as my instincts and his, and told me to come in the next morning so he could take my daughter by C-section.

As soon as I came in the next morning, the doctor was ready. Before anyone had time to test for contractions, he said, "I'm taking her in for surgery."

Samantha was born soon after, safe and healthy. The first gift this doctor gave me was a healthy daughter. The second gift was the fact that he trusted me—he understood a mother's intuition. The fact that a *man* was acknowledging my truth wasn't lost on me either. It had been a long time since I'd spoken my truth to a man who had believed me wholeheartedly.

With Sam's birth, the fog lifted even more. The more awake and confident I was feeling, the stronger my calling to make changes in my life. I had listened to my body, and I finally started listening to my own knowing.

FOUR SMALL HINGES

I had studied nutrition and fitness in college, and I had been working as a personal trainer since then, but I didn't fully understand the power of food until I experienced the earth-shattering loss of my son. It was through the process of putting myself back together that I had my *aha* moment: Movement will heal me, healing food will awaken my spirit, and the words I speak to myself will determine my future.

I love the phrase "Small hinges move big doors." It means that small, daily positive actions can create enormous momentum in changing your overall life and future. My first small acts, my first hinges, focused on the physical, which, in turn, impacted the mental and spiritual.

First Hinge: Healing Movement

The quickest way to alter your state is by moving—any type of movement will do. Walking, dancing, stretching, or a good lift session can shift your mental, physical, and emotional states in an instant. When you move, you pump blood into your cells, which in essence wakes up your soul, helping you tap into your cellular knowings and rememberings.

Our bodies and the ability to move them to stir the soul have been our gift from the moment we were born. Movement allows us to clear out cobwebs in our minds, hearts, and souls. Movement has been and always will be our gift to tap into our knowing, our remembrance of our greatness, and our truth. With more than 20 years of experience as a fitness professional, I have watched client after client become more empowered, happier, and more grounded through movement.

It's so helpful, and so simple—and yet, so often, we just don't do it. It isn't that we don't know what to do when it comes to movement. It usually is that we allow our egos to get in the way, and we convince ourselves that we are simply *too busy.* We say we are too tired. We fall into the victim role that we—especially those who get their butts out of bed at 5:30 A.M.—are even more tired than everyone else. We use other body parts as an excuse. "I have a bum shoulder and can't work out." Sometimes we use our busy schedule or even our family as an excuse as to why we can't fit even a small amount of movement into each day. Yet we make ample time to binge-watch our favorite TV shows, or to spend an hour scrolling through social media before bed.

Too many of us are waiting until we feel like it. You *will* start to feel like it after you let your spirit win over your ego every single time, over and over and over again.

It doesn't matter *how* you move your body. It just matters that you *do*. We get caught up looking for the *right* workout when the right workout is whatever lights us up and allows us to feel good when it's over.

Ideas for movement:

1. Walk. Put on your shoes and simply walk out your door. While you walk, notice the trees, the sky, the sounds of the animals. Smell the air and say a prayer.
2. Dance. Turn on your favorite song and move like nobody is watching. Better yet, grab your kids or your spouse and have a dance-off party in the kitchen!
3. Flow. In the Resources section, I provide a link to a beautiful flow workout that is easy and allows you to feel peace instantly.*
4. High-intensity interval training. Do you need a good sweat session? Do you want to feel alive? During my hardest times, high-intensity interval training workouts would make me feel alive, powerful, and just for a moment, like I had it all together. I've got a HIIT workout for you—one that allows you to *feel*.*

Second Hinge: Healing Foods

The food we put in our bodies has the ability to heal, to reverse disease and aging, and to increase vitality, energy, and feel-good hormones. The saying "Let food be thy medicine" is so true. Like movement, food can have profound effects on our overall well-being.

Food that is *living*, meaning organic and as unprocessed as possible, awakens the cells. Food that grows naturally in nature awakens the cells. Real food that grows in healthy soil and is kissed by the sun is alive. It has a high cellular frequency and vibration, which awakens your cells and helps you tap into your soul.

I believe if we eat what is naturally grown versus what is produced in a manufacturing plant, we can dramatically reverse aging, illness, lethargy, and depression. Mother Nature provides medicine in our foods. We have all the tastes we need from nature through spices, fruits, vegetables, fats, and protein sources.

Don't underestimate the power of healing food to dramatically change your mental, emotional, and physical state. It took this downfall, my dark night of the soul, for me to really understand the power of food and the power of movement.

When we have toxins in our organs, which most everyone does, it slows down our metabolism, creates excess body fat to protect the organs, and creates disease, sluggishness, skin disorders, and anxiety. When you consume healing foods, you release these toxins from your system and revitalize your cells with nutrients that rebalance the hormones and create homeostasis in the body.

Most people are surprised to experience the impact that one day of a detox* can have on their system. It really does only take one day to feel lighter, more energized, and less bloated—and, most important, to have more hope.

Third Hinge: Nature

Nature is in constant vibration. Nature is the reminder that we are connected to something higher than ourselves. It allows us to feel so big and powerful, yet so small and dependent at the same time.

Being with nature is a small thing that you can do every single day, even if you don't have access to the wilderness of a forest, an expansive mountain, or a peaceful body of water. You can always feel the breeze on your face, or feel the sun warm your skin. You can touch a tree or sit under one for a few minutes to experience the shade it provides. Don't be afraid to take off your shoes and walk in the dirt and grass.

In fact, there's scientific evidence that this grounding, or earthing, is healing to your body! According to a study published in the *Journal of Environmental and Public Health*, "Reconnection with the Earth's electrons has been found to promote intriguing physiological changes and subjective reports of well-being . . . including better sleep and reduced pain."

Another way to be in touch with nature is to bring the outside indoors. Select a few plants to keep in your home or office. Not only will they help purify the air, but they will provide a gentle and beautiful reminder that you are never alone.

Crystals and stones can be used for decoration and in meditation. Wearing jewelry with authentic gemstones from nature can provide a sense of peace, energy, or even empowerment. Salt lamps, when placed in areas of your home where there are electronics, can also help to purify the air and stabilize your mood throughout the day.

These are all reminders that you are connected to something higher. We all have this cellular knowing, that we are connected to everyone and everything, and that we each hold infinite intelligence and infinite wisdom within us.

Fourth Hinge: Healing Words

Speaking and hearing loving words are small acts that move big doors. The power of speaking positive words out loud and in your mind may sound corny, but it, too, is backed by science. According to Andrew Newberg, M.D., and Mark Robert Waldman in their book *Words Can Change Your Brain*, "A single word has the power to influence the expression of genes that regulate physical and emotional stress."[2] The work of telling yourself kind things over and over and rewiring your mind will, in essence, get your body going in that same direction. On the other hand, a negative spoken word will increase the activity in the fear center of the brain, which can interrupt our brain functions, distract us from the task at hand, and cause our mood to sour instantly.

Newberg and Waldman write, "Angry words send alarm messages through the brain, and they partially shut down the logic-and-reasoning centers located in the frontal lobes . . . By holding a positive and optimistic thought in your mind, you stimulate frontal lobe activity, [and] other areas of the brain. Over time the structure of your thalamus will . . . change in response to your conscious words, thoughts, and feelings, [affecting] the way in which you perceive reality."[3]

You literally have the power to create joy or sadness—success or failure—for yourself and others with the words you choose.

Affirmations take a while to get used to. Sometimes you can feel good after you say them, and sometimes you don't feel any different and then you feel like you're lying to yourself. You have to continue, whether you feel like it or not. You're going to talk to yourself all day every day anyway—you might as well do yourself a huge favor and make those *nice words*.

It's true that we have negativity raging in our heads 24/7. In fact, humans are hardwired for negativity, mistrust, and problem-solving. It's part of our survival skill set. For me, negativity was raging all the time. *I am not a good mother. I am a financial ruin. I am not living my truth. I am ugly. I am not successful. I am not making a difference. I am not worthy. I am not enough.*

I started with those mean and nasty words, and had to grow upward. I had to start speaking the complete opposite of those nasty thoughts to myself daily—sometimes every 15 minutes! *I AM a great mother. I AM a financial success. I AM living my truth. I AM beautiful. I AM extremely successful. I AM making a huge difference. I AM worthy. I AM more than enough.*

If you are new to positive affirmations, you can follow along on a guided affirmation with me.*

In those early moments after my depression, I was just starting to bring a little more light, life, and hope into my life every single day, with a little bit more truth unfolding, releasing what no longer served me, and with less negativity raging in my mind. I might have done only *one* of those things each day, but my momentum started with that—one choice, one act to move me into the world I live in today.

Every day, when you make one choice, you are freeing yourself to own your brilliance, your light, your truth, your power. It won't happen overnight. But all you have to do is take one step forward.

What is one thing you can do daily to get a different outcome?

What is your soul asking you to do more of?

In which ways can you add movement, writing, reading, silence, or healing foods to your life?

CHAPTER 4

Enlightenment in a Bikini

Courage is the most important of all the virtues, because without courage you can't practice any other virtue consistently.

— MAYA ANGELOU

When I got the crazy idea to enter the World's Bikini Competition in Toronto, Canada, Samantha was only a few months old and my marriage was barely existent.

I had always been brought up to cover my body— completely. To do otherwise was shameful. My very religious upbringing taught me that modesty is a prized virtue. I received a pamphlet at age 12 about what was appropriate to wear and what was not; wearing anything above the knees, or even a tank top, was considered immodest. I had a belief system of shame around my body and showing any skin, so I wore long skirts and long sleeves. A bikini was *out of the question*.

I had played sports my entire life and I trained people in the gym. Apart from the sports I participated in and regular training, I didn't know how to move my body in any other way. I'd never danced before, I sure didn't like sex, I wasn't comfortable yet with the idea of being sensual, and I didn't know how to walk or carry myself in a more self-aware and confident way.

But I was feeling more confident, and I wanted to act on that. I wanted to do something I'd never done before, something that scared me to death. While it was terrifying and a little naughty to do something *forbidden*, I followed the butterflies in my belly.

I'd heard stories about bikini and fitness competitors putting their bodies through hell in order to appear their best. I had just gone through my personal transformation to become healthier, making the small but positive choices of eating clean, moving my body, and working on my mind. I wanted to see if I could create a bikini competition–worthy body using my meal plan of healing foods, in addition to my movement plan.

When I started doing these small-hinge movements, I began tapping into my soul. And while it seems crazy that my soul would say something like, "Enter a bikini competition," that is truly what I heard. Honestly, our souls can tell us to do a lot of seemingly crazy things—I guess they have a sense of humor! Mine was leading me to my edge—an edge that would be a tipping point for a rewrite of my entire life.

There were just a few obstacles:

One: Participating in a bikini competition meant *I had to wear a bikini*. I'd never worn one before and I would have to wear one onstage in front of hundreds of strangers. Two: I had *never* walked in high heels—ever. I didn't even own a pair. I was certain I would fall on my butt. Three: I didn't have a lot of extra money, which was required for both entrance into the competition and to buy the swimwear. Because these weren't off-the-hanger two-pieces from Walmart. No. The handmade bikinis these ladies wore onstage were made with sequins and nice fabrics and usually cost around $1,000 *each*.

Nothing scared me more. So . . . I did it!

PEELING BACK THE LAYERS

Signing the paper to enter the bikini competition was a very deliberate choice and led me on a three-month journey of getting control of my life, stepping into fear, and being proactive about the life I wanted to create. I could have chosen to do a local or state competition, but I wanted to do World's, because I knew I wouldn't be able to turn back. Money was a big factor because I had a scarcity mind-set. I was always making decisions around how much money I spent or how little money I had. Laying down the entry fee for the World's Bikini Competition in Toronto, Canada, as well as paying for the flight and hotel—these things were not cheap. But I *had* to put myself on the line financially or I knew I wouldn't go through with it. Go big or go home!

The trouble was, I didn't know anything about bikini competitions. None of the women I knew had ever done such a thing, and I had no idea what to do to prepare for it. But my soul knew. My soul understood the unlayering that would be required from such a seemingly frivolous event.

Here's the thing: Not only did I know that my family and everyone I knew would judge me for such a thing, *I* judged myself, too! I thought people who did fitness competitions were shallow and insecure. My soul knew better and knew that those judgments needed to be uncovered and cast aside. It said, "This thing will terrify you, and you must do the very thing that you judged. You must unlayer stories around your body, your beliefs, and the judgments you have placed on others and yourself."

I looked into where I could get a sequined swimsuit, and I watched countless hours of ladies walking onstage while my girls slept. Just as I feared, I read story after story about women who competed in bikini competitions, fitness competitions, and muscle competitions, who were depriving themselves. They were taking laxatives, limiting water, and not eating. Their hair was falling out. They were getting acne. They were angry all the time. They would go into a rage for the smallest reasons. Their plans for success were built on deprivation, but I didn't want to deprive myself *at all*. I wanted to celebrate and nurture myself! I wanted to prove that eating healing foods six times a day and moving your body five times a week could do just as good a job, if not better, at creating a healthy, lean, sexy body.

So I continued eating healing foods that were nutrient-dense up to six times a day, using the meal plans that I had developed—the same plans that I share today with my clients. I was committed to these healing foods! And as I stuck with that goal and those daily actions, my spirit was soaring. I was feeling more confident. And I had more energy than ever before.

My body was shifting and changing, too. I started taking better care of my skin by using exfoliants and sunscreen. My skin was clearing up and looking younger every single day. I was moving my body with a commitment to feed it with the best exercise, to take care of it, and to rest up to eight hours a day. However, I had two children, a hectic work schedule, and a husband who seemed to still be operating in denial. I could control my food and exercise, but not the sleep cycle of my six-month-old. There were many times when I had to keep moving forward even though I didn't adhere to my plan perfectly.

My mind had to match up with what I was about to embark on, so I picked up *The Power of Intention* by Wayne Dyer. That book opened me up to the power of my mind, the power of my choice through intention, and the power of my visualizations. I started putting this knowledge into practice and began to visualize and declare daily affirmations about creating whatever I put my mind to.

I learned I needed to set an intention, and I decided my intention was to place in the top 10. Remember: *Go big or go home.* I also had an intention of showing people that you can achieve your goals *without* deprivation. Although I didn't know it at the time, I was the first woman to enter this competition without any other competitions under her belt.

I knew I could do great things with clean eating and with self-love. I was fairly confident I could achieve my goals. But there was still problem number two: I had to learn how to walk in heels.

LEARNING HOW TO WALK AGAIN

I went down to the local Walmart to pick up my first pair of high heels. I strapped those cheap, plastic high heels on, determined to practice, but unlike a lot of women, *I did not feel powerful.* My ankles were wobbling so much I was worried I would sprain an ankle. As my feet were crunched into the toes of the shoes, I wondered why women wear high heels at all! I knew it was mandatory, because high heels are known to make your calves look better and create a nice curve in your lower back. So, I committed to practicing every day, even if I initially looked like a clumsy giraffe.

I practiced in my kitchen, putting on a show for my daughters, who thought it was great fun to sit and watch me click back and forth on the wood floor. After 20 minutes, my feet ached. I felt absolutely ridiculous! But I got better and better. I watched YouTube videos, taking mental notes of how women walked on the catwalk, how they would step one foot and cross in front of the other, creating a nice little sway of the hip. I definitely needed to work on that. *We did not sway or sashay in my religion.*

I had been a basketball player, so my walk was very boxy. Swaying was a very difficult concept for me and felt uncomfortable. But my learning to walk in high heels was just a physical manifestation of the kind of *uncomfortable* I was in all areas of myself. I was making an effort to choose people and circumstances that were uncomfortable—and believe me, nothing made me more uncomfortable than this competition!

One day, I realized that my kitchen was not big enough, and I needed a longer area to continue walking in these high heels, so I went outside and walked up and down the sidewalk on our street. I imagine many of our neighbors were looking out their windows wondering, *Who is this lady wearing high heels, shorts, and a baggy shirt, walking back and forth in front of her house?*

I'd come a long way from those dark times, when I felt physically unable to leave the house. Now, striding back and forth in front of my house in broad daylight, I no longer cared what the neighbors might think or who might see me.

Shedding Old Support Systems and Beliefs

I didn't just shed body fat and fear as I stepped into this new calling—I shed paradigms, stories, and beliefs that no longer served me. One was that a bikini was immodest. Two was that most women who competed in bikini contests were shallow and in need of validation. Instead, I stepped into different truths: that I could do something new without any support—and that when I put my mind and soul into something, I would follow through to the end.

As a mom of two girls, I had to ask myself, *What is the message I am sharing with them? Am I teaching them that their value lies in standing on a stage in a bikini?*

I struggled to find the true answer to that, as I had always believed that the only reason any woman got onstage in a bikini was to receive validation. But in the end, I accepted my truth: I wasn't doing this to get validation for myself or to receive value. I was doing this to *step into radical fear.* I was stepping onstage as a sign that I valued myself, to prove that despite all my imperfections and inexperience, I could follow through with something that terrified me. I was doing this purely for me, to see if I could follow through with my soul's calling, even when it didn't make any sense. Perhaps *particularly* when it didn't make any sense.

It was not lost on me that to physically unlayer my clothing down to a bikini served as a perfect metaphor for my entire life: I was basically stripping myself naked to expose my vulnerability, to the truth of who I was, albeit to a roomful of strangers.

Unexpected Kindness

I had my nutrition and fitness in check. I was saying my daily affirmations and focusing on my intention. I'd even gotten really good (I thought) at walking in high heels. But I couldn't turn to any of the family or friends who had been my support system in the past. I couldn't even tell any of them about the competition because they wouldn't have approved.

I really needed an ally—someone to help me prepare for the competition.

I found a group that helps people get ready for bikini competitions and reached out to them, but I couldn't afford their coaching. They gave me the name of a woman, Stephanie Jacobs, who lived in my town. She had competed and done well in a lot of bikini competitions, and they suggested I might be able to pay her for private lessons. That was more money I didn't have, but I gave her a call anyway.

A few days later, I pulled into her subdivision in a nicer neighborhood in Salt Lake City. Walking to the front door of her exquisite home, I was thinking, *This lady is out of my league. She* plants *and* grows *flowers. Any woman who has a beautiful garden in her front yard has got it all together. She is going to look at me, shut the door, and I am going to have no one to help me on this journey.* But my soul must have known that she was going to be an angel in disguise. She was going to help me awaken in many areas of my life.

I knocked, and a beautiful woman answered the door.

"Come on in," she said. We went to her private home gym, and I saw she had everything I'd need to train. I hadn't even had time to compliment her on her beautiful home when she said, "I will help you." She was offering to coach me for free, which seemed foreign to me, because you always have to pay something to get something, right? (This was one of many beliefs Stephanie helped me to shatter in time.) Even though I felt sure there had to be a catch, I accepted right away and we agreed to meet once a week.

Then came the first challenge. After realizing we wore the same shoe size, she handed me a pair of heels and told me to try them on. This was my moment! I had been practicing in high heels every day and I was excited to show her just how well I could walk. I put on the high heels and strutted through her gym back and forth, under her watchful eye.

"I am going to be honest with you," she said with a kind smile. "You need a lot of work. Have you taken dance classes?"

Of course I hadn't. She suggested I do Zumba to learn how to move my hips and my body, to become less stiff and more comfortable with my own femininity.

We sat around her kitchen table, and she asked me what I was eating. I started to map out what I was eating and when, sharing my meal plan and the use of superfoods with her. It was all very practical. I don't know how the conversation took a turn from there—we barely knew each other—but I will always remember the words that came out of her mouth next.

She had lost her son when he was two years old. He was in the backyard on the swing set, and she was inside when it happened. My mind was swimming. Did she feel the guilt that I had felt, too? My heart ached for her loss. *I knew the pain she felt.* It was all I could do not to burst into tears, my emotions were so raw.

She had carried that story with her for many years. So there, at my new friend's kitchen table, I shared my story with her, too. When we found out we both had lost our sons, we bonded instantly over the pain and the recognition that we were no longer alone in our pain. *Someone else understood.*

It was a beautiful moment we had as sisters, a moment of radical truth-telling, a moment of vulnerability. I knew she could see my breakdown and my struggle, and she could see I was not yet on the other side. I remember distinctly knowing in my cells that I was not there for her to just help me with this bikini competition. I was there to hear her story. I was there to *know* and deeply understand that I was not alone and neither was she. After that conversation, we were equally invested in my goal.

When Stephanie's awakening came, it also began with movement and with yoga. She started entering bikini competitions after her loss, and she told me how they began to free her and help open her mind to her power and to who she was. Coming from a trainer's background, I understood the power that arises from women who start lifting weights. Time and time again, I would watch women who signed up with a trainer and stayed committed to that trainer, to themselves, and to their goals. Their bodies would transform, and their muscles would start to increase, and their shape would change, but more than that, their minds and confidence changed, too. There was a new power in the way they stood and the truth they embraced.

Moments later, Stephanie brought out a beautiful sequined bikini that easily cost $1,000 and looked like it would fit my seven-year-old daughter. I didn't have

$1,000. And I was bigger than a seven-year-old. Still, she said, "Try this on."

I trudged into the bathroom, thinking there was no way this thing would fit me. I was going to have the ultimate camel toe. I slipped into the sequined contraption, looked in the mirror, and thought, *This does not fit me.* This itty-bitty bikini was exposing all my womanly parts!

I walked out and tried to laugh it off. "This is too small," I said. In reality, I felt embarrassed, and completely exposed.

She grabbed the thin fabric at my hip and cinched up the sides, exposing my rear end even more, and said, "This cups you perfectly, see?" Then she adjusted a little bit of the bra top and she said with a big smile, "This is perfect!"

Why did I sign up for this? How does she think this fits me? My butt cheeks were hanging out! My vulnerability was raging. There was nothing left to the imagination, and I knew *this* was what it was going to feel like. And I was going to walk out onto a stage and have my body broadcast on ESPN?

We Get There How We Get There

I never expected my spirit to rise higher in a bikini, or that I would experience the unconditional sisterly support from another woman in the process. Stephanie's support meant everything to me, and gave me the confidence I could not have found otherwise.

As I proceeded to practice walking in the bikini and high heels that Stephanie had gladly given me, and worked toward feeling comfortable—even excited—about shedding my clothes on a national stage, I was able to shed some of my limitations in other areas as well.

Our souls' callings can come in many forms. Transformation doesn't always look like crystals around your neck, a daily meditation practice, or chanting *om* for 10 minutes straight. Our job is to be on the lookout and listen to our own drum, our own whisperings, our own soul nudgings. My soul was calling for me to unlayer— old patterns, stories, and beliefs—and stand naked and vulnerable in my truth.

I flew to Canada the day before the competition. I didn't know much about makeup, but these massive competitions have an on-site makeup artist, and the women file in starting at 4 A.M. to get their makeup done. There's also a room designated for a massive line of spray tanning.

There was a long assembly line of women out the door of this hotel room to bring them in, spray them down, and get them out. A bunch of us were shoved in the bathroom to wait—and all the women started stripping down naked. But I had never exposed my body in front of anyone before, except my husband, and that was usually in the dark. I was unprepared for the deluge of thoughts! *Why are we stripping down? I don't want to show my body. Why are you showing me your body? Oh, my gosh, your boobs are so perky and your body is so perfect. I hope they don't notice that I cannot stop staring.*

We stepped out of the bathroom, and my clothes were still on. When it was my turn, the lady looked at me, holding the bottle of spray tan in her hand, and squawked, "Why aren't your clothes off?"

I wanted to go around the corner to take off my clothes, and she rolled her eyes like I was taking up a lot of time—she was going to see me naked anyway, so why did it matter *where* I got naked? I was holding up the line.

I quickly disrobed and stood there naked and afraid, and she sprayed me. I had never been that dark or shiny or sticky before. I put my clothes back on and ran out of the room. All the other girls were chitchatting, laughing, having a great time, and here I was—completely vulnerable, completely alone.

The next morning, I got up early to get my makeup done. I did my hair the best I could, with as much curl and as much hairspray as I could manage. I was nervous and rushing to get ready, but it wasn't quite real until I slipped into that sequined bikini.

This was it! This was my moment. And I was scared to death.

Don't fall. Smile big, pop your booty, and breathe! You've got this, girl! Top 10! I kept pep-talking myself all the way from the dressing rooms to the back of the auditorium.

Before we were called onstage, we all waited in the back and I could finally get a look at everyone. There were more than 100 girls in my category, and every single one of them looked like they would win. I didn't know how the judges could possibly pick who would win this competition, because there was no differentiator! They all seemed flawless. The doubts and fear snuck in as I stood there in my itty-bitty bikini with my number pinned to it, thinking I was a fool and this was not my kind of sport. I'd waited for this day for months—it was supposed to be *my big day*—and I could not wait for it to end.

Dang it. I was not honoring what my soul was calling me to do. I was allowing doubt, and fear, and all those stories and beliefs and judgments to creep back in.

I took a deep breath, steadied my racing heart, and focused on the power of intention. What was my "why"? Why was I here? What was my truth? I was going to stand on that stage, not because I needed validation from any one of those judges, but because I needed validation from myself. I needed to know that I could complete something totally out of my wheelhouse. I needed to know that I could do this without starving myself, without doing it the way everybody else did it. I needed to know I could do this without anyone in the audience to encourage me or cheer me on like all the other women had. I needed to prove that I could survive and even thrive without the support and approval of my family and friends.

I needed to unlayer all the many, many stories that were holding me back from my happiness—the stories that said I wasn't good enough or a good mom, that I was immodest, unholy, going to hell, a financial ruin, and was never going to make a difference in the world. That my truth and intentions didn't matter.

I was ready to unlayer all of that. I was done with it all.

But I was terrified. I felt like everyone around me knew the routine and knew what was happening. Since this was my first competition, all this lining up, standing around, and waiting to go onstage was so foreign to me. I was watching everyone to look for cues, and finally I had to ask the girls standing next to me what I was supposed to do!

Right before my number was called to walk out onstage, I held on to my intention like Wayne Dyer talked about. I visualized what I wanted to happen and I went for it. I didn't know anyone in the crowd. In fact, each girl there had at least one if not a handful of people there cheering her on. I had no one. It was only me, the stage, the judges, and my intention to place in the top 10.

As our group of numbers was gathered together, I took off my robe and I stood in near nakedness. I was not ashamed of my body. In fact, I was *proud* of my body and all the hard work it took to get there. I held on to my "why" and I held on to my intention. Then they called my number.

I walked to the front of the stage, and I held on to that "Fake it till you make it" smile. I rolled my shoulders back. I tilted my back to pop my booty out. I walked the best that I had ever walked in those high heels. But one thing gave me away, and it was the one thing that gave me away every single time.

Ordinarily I could hide behind my long pants or my skirt, but here I was fully exposed, and skin on my knees started to vibrate and shake like it always does when I am nervous. I knew they were moving, and there was no way the judges were not going to see my fear, no matter how big my smile, how poufy my hair, or how tan my body was. My vulnerability and my fear were exposed. And I could do nothing but stand there and smile.

We exited the stage from our first round and waited for the finals, which was for the top 25. When my number was called, I could not believe it.

The second time, I stepped onstage with a little more confidence, with a little more knowing, and a little more pride that *I had done it*, that I had carried through and stepped into my fear one day at a time. I stood with 24 other girls, knees still knocking, skin still shaking, but something in my heart felt at ease.

As we stood onstage, the top 10 winners were announced, and my number was called again! The ESPN announcers couldn't believe that somebody in the top 10 had never done a competition before and actually placed.

They were making a big deal about it, which made me feel even better.

I left that stage a winner, as far as I was concerned. I had achieved my original intention of being in the top 10, and I had done it on my own terms.

As all the other competitors pulled out their boxes of donuts and all the food they had deprived themselves of over the last few months, I didn't feel that desire. I didn't feel like I had been depriving myself of anything—I had *given myself something.*

Finding a quiet bathroom down the hall, I stood in front of the mirror and looked at myself—and I didn't recognize myself at all. There was so much makeup on my face that I didn't look like *me.*

I took off my fake eyelashes and started to slowly wipe off my makeup, one streak at a time, finally exposing my raw face and my pale blue eyes, without all the glitter and glam.

It felt so good and empowering that I couldn't help but smile.

In that moment, I was looking at a girl who looked more beautiful without her makeup and layers than she did with them on. I knew that there was more to this than just a bikini competition. I was on a path of deep transformation, because for the first time in a very long time, I loved the girl staring back at me.

LISTENING IN THE SILENCE

After the high, there is always the stillness, that gap of nothingness. During the months while I was preparing, I was spiritually and emotionally waking up more and more each day. And now, in the silence, I heard and truly acknowledged my soul telling me that my marital relationship wasn't right for me.

I was in the kitchen cooking dinner. I had only just returned from Canada, and having learned and grown so much from trusting my soul's voice, I wanted to keep going on that path . . . but this was *hard*. As hard as the bikini competition had been, the idea of leaving my husband was terrifying.

My soul was asking me to tell my husband the truth. I wasn't okay with my lack of trust in him. I wasn't okay with pretending like I was happy. I wasn't going to put up with these fake identities that he was putting on, and the lies and moods that he was going through. I was going to own my truth and speak my truth. Having been so brave and empowered, I couldn't continue to come home to a life spent in a lie.

But what about the girls? Will they feel like I broke up the only home they know? Will they resent me? Will I be letting them down if I decide to leave Laerer?

I thought about how fun and sweet Laerer was when Sarah was born. *Why couldn't it have stayed that way?*

But no. There were signs it wasn't working even back then. I was just ignoring them because I was wrapped up in being a new mom.

I thought back to my wedding day, when I was certain I didn't want to get married but I did it anyway. I couldn't help but wonder what my life would have been like if I hadn't married Laerer. I'd once dreamed of being an archaeologist and traveling the world. In fact, I had wanted to join the Peace Corps instead of getting married, but I wanted to be *good* more than I wanted to listen to my own voice.

No, I should have never married Laerer. But if I hadn't, I wouldn't have my daughters. They were and are my greatest teachers. They made me a mom and made me stronger than I ever thought I could be.

My girls meant everything to me. And I was about to disrupt their world.

Every woman who finds herself in a difficult relationship has to make this decision sooner or later: Do I step into this relationship and give a little bit more? Or do I step away? I knew I had given everything I had. And I also had to be honest with myself: My kids were my number-one priority, and the only thing keeping Laerer and me together was our kids.

There in the kitchen, I took a deep breath and decided to get a divorce. I decided to follow the beating of my own heart, to be the kind of mom that I wanted to be and not the mom that I was told I needed to be, and be successful in the way that I wanted to be successful, even if it looked different than what was expected of me.

LISTENING TO MY SOUL OVER ALL THE NOISE

I had to learn to be my own rescuer. I had to be my biggest influence.

I was finally choosing to be my own best friend, to love myself as hard as I wanted someone else to love me, in all my dimensions, all my rawness, and all my craziness. I wanted to be soft, but I also wanted to be a badass in business. I wanted to be that nurturing, always-there mama, and I wanted to be free, traveling the world. I wanted to be a gentle and supportive wife, but I also wanted to be that fierce, passionate, fiery lover. I wanted to be religious and spiritual, but I also wanted to be a little edgy and raw. I wanted to be sad and I wanted to be happy. I wanted it all.

I had made up my mind.

In the moment of quiet after the girls went to bed, I gathered all the courage in my body and told Laerer how I felt—all of it. It wasn't easy, but the more I spoke my truths out loud to him, the more confidence and peace I felt in my decision. I was honoring the beat of my heart. My soul. My one true friend. I wanted to get a separation, file for divorce, and move into radical healing.

I thought there might be a chance that Laerer would understand. He hadn't seemed happy for a long time, so maybe he would be relieved. I also thought this was going to be very amicable.

It was not.

Insights on Enlightenment

Growth and enlightenment do not come in a one-size-fits-all package. I used to think that kind of thing only happened after sitting in meditation in a cave for hours on end, or by going to some high-end transformational retreat in Costa Rica where you do yoga in the treetops with monkeys. I certainly did not expect a bikini competition to be a major stepping-stone on my path to transformation. I just knew that I was being called to do it.

When you step into something that terrifies you and you take a stand for your own interests—especially when you don't receive any outside support—that act gives you permission to step into other things for which you might not have received support, either. Getting out of your comfort zone expands your capacity to live and your container for life, because you just proved to yourself you could do this thing and survive.

For me, the competition was a stepping-stone of confidence. I didn't fall. I stuck with it. I was grateful to myself for doing something just for me. And because I did it and survived, it made me think, *Where else in my life can I make it into the top 10? Where else can I stand onstage? Where else in my life can I take having the spotlight on me? What other areas can I completely unlayer and then reconstruct according to what feels true for me now? Where else can I stand naked, and raw, and vulnerable—and still show up?*

The beauty of enlightenment is that it is a process based on growth. It can show up in a million different ways. It is not an endgame. It is not something you reach and then you're there forever. It's a daily illumination of the dark parts of your soul and an opportunity to grow in each endeavor you take on.

Where in your life were you uncomfortable, or scared, but you stepped in regardless?

Where in your life did you display courage when it wasn't popular?

Where else can you stand naked, and raw, and vulnerable—and still show up?

CHAPTER 5

The Year of Divine Awakening

I am blooming from the wound where I once bled.

— RUNE LAZULI

Family is the priority in the Church of Latter-Day Saints. Divorce was not something you did, especially to the nice guy, especially to the guy who went to church, especially to the guy who helped make dinner at night, who helped bag sandwiches, and who mourned with you when your baby died. Laerer and I were already separated. Due to our financial situation, the church provided us with a counselor to try and help us work through our challenges and save our marriage.

Thus I was shocked when one day about a month into our counseling sessions, she grabbed my arm, leaned in close, and said, "I'm not allowed to share details with you, but you need to get out and go check your bank accounts. Make sure you get primary custody of your kids. You need to pull up your big-girl panties and you need to get out of this relationship right now."

I was taken aback. I had no idea what to think.

She knew details I didn't. The counselor was genuinely concerned for my well-being, and I was caught completely off guard that the very person who was there to save my marriage was indeed telling me to run.

I'd assumed that even though we were getting a divorce, I didn't have to worry about Laerer doing anything mean or vindictive. After all, he was a financial planner and he had assured me everything would be fine. I believed we could do everything amicably. I was delusional.

I didn't immediately flee like the counselor told me to. I needed to think, to absorb what she was telling me. And so I just went about my day. My girls and I ran errands, and we went to the grocery store. I swiped my credit card at the register, but it was denied. *Strange*, I thought. I pulled out another card and swiped again. It was also denied. Now I was getting worried. I had one more card left and swiped it, hoping there had been a glitch in the system. It was also denied.

Despite the counselor's warning, I didn't immediately understand why. I was the primary breadwinner—the one with the stable job—and I knew I had money in my account.

Humiliated and bewildered, I gathered my two little girls and left the groceries sitting in my cart. This was not an accident. I did not have three faulty credit cards. I loaded the girls back into the car and immediately drove to the bank.

My husband had moved out a few months back. We hadn't seen much of him—he wasn't participating with the girls, and I assumed he was taking time to adjust to the situation. On the few occasions we did talk, I could feel the anger and rage rising within him, but I had no idea he could ever do something like this.

Our bank had a table set up with coffee and hot chocolate for customers. I forced a smile, and told my girls to head over to the hot chocolate table, that I just needed to do this one more errand and we could go home. Once they were happily occupied, I sat down at the desk with the teller. As calmly as I could, I explained that I had just tried to buy groceries and that none of my credit cards were working.

The teller pulled up my account while I waited with a pit in my stomach. Maybe it was all a big mistake.

No. Actually, it was worse than I'd thought. The teller informed me that I had *seven* accounts, all opened by my husband. And they were all empty.

At my frantic request to dig deeper, she said some of the money had been removed from our joint accounts slowly and surely, *all the way back to two years prior.*

"Is there anything you can do?" I pleaded. "I never gave permission for any of this money to be withdrawn." There was nothing she could do. It didn't matter where the money went or who took it if there were two signatures on the account. He didn't need two signatures to zero out an account. Just one—his.

The teller started listing off the names of the accounts, and when she said the words "Children's Savings Green," my stomach sank. My thoughts went to Sarah, my oldest daughter. Even though we barely had any money when she was born, we were dedicated to putting $50 in this savings account every month so that by the time she graduated from college, or by the time she had the dream to pursue a business or a mission beating in her heart, she would have the funds to go after it. When Samantha was born, we did the same thing. This was for their hopes. This was for their dreams. This was a gift that would set them apart and give them a head start. These were funds we were *never* going to touch.

They were gone. My husband had stolen from our children.

I looked over at my two little girls. They smiled their big, gummy smiles at me with their chocolate-stained lips, stirring their chocolate cups. Their innocence and happiness gave me strength. We were going to find a way to buy groceries and survive with nothing. Laerer could steal our money, but I would not allow him to steal our joy.

Holding a smile for their sake, I told them it was time to go, though everything inside my gut was turning. I buckled them into their car seats and got in. With perfect timing, my youngest said, "Mommy, I'm hungry."

I did not have groceries. I did not have money in my account to buy groceries.

In that moment, I realized there was nothing separating me from anyone else who felt deprived of money or deprived of the ability to take care of their own children.

I didn't ask anyone for money. In my depleted low state, asking for money would be admitting that I had failed. I wasn't able to *feed* my children, the most basic task for any mother. I was in financial ruin. I had married the wrong person. I had somehow created his rage and I had gotten us into this situation.

I did a mental scan of my kitchen and knew I had a few packaged boxes and a few canned goods. That would have to do. After dinner, I proposed a game: "We're going to look under every piece of furniture, overturn every couch cushion, and see how much money we can come up with, and whoever finds the most money wins!" In less than an hour, the pile of change we had totaled $47.63. That's all I had to my name.

Soon after, I slept on a mattress on the floor. Samantha was still in her crib, and I gave my oldest daughter Sarah the nicest furniture in the house—a queen-size bed my dad had handmade out of pinewood as my wedding gift. I wanted her to have the nicest piece of furniture in our home and to be able to crawl up in that big queen bed and feel like a princess, especially if I didn't. Tinfoil held our TV together to get two child-friendly channels, one of which was the PBS station so my little girls could watch *Curious George* and *Clifford the Big Red Dog.*

We sold everything else. Groceries were more important than furniture.

I tried to tell myself we had everything we really needed, but I still felt I was letting my kids down. What kind of example was I setting as a mother? What was I teaching my children? I wondered if I was going to crawl out of this situation, or if this would be my lot in life. Would I be single, sleeping on the floor, forever?

My Second Rock Bottom

It was official: I was at my second rock bottom.

I wasn't associating with my husband's family. My relationship with my own family was on the rocks. They were questioning me, my relationship with God, and they blamed me for my current situation. Even though we had agreed not to tell them about the bikini competition, Laerer had gone behind my back and told them anyway, knowing it was something they would never approve of. Needless to say, they were horrified.

My parents cried for me. They were worried for me, my welfare, my mental capacity, and my spiritual well-being. What would ever possess me to reveal my body on a stage in front of other people? If I felt compelled to do *that*, then divorce and possibly leaving my children must be next . . . and then drugs, and then alcoholism, and then God knows what. This is how the mind can work. This is where they were going.

And when Laerer spread the lies the counselor told me about, my parents believed him. And broke my heart.

I didn't have many friends and I wasn't going to share my personal defeats with my clients, although I did start asking them to pay for a package of sessions up front instead of spacing it out over several months. That at least gave me money for bills and groceries for the next few weeks.

But there was a hidden blessing in all of this. With the lack of people coming in and out of my home, the lack of friends, and the lack of constant TV, there was instead a stillness. I now had an opportunity to hear my own heart beat and to listen to my own voice. I remembered all the times when my inner voice—my spirit, my soul—had spoken to me, and I was now able to hear it again.

I had so much shame, so much rage, and so much sorrow for what had become of my life and my daughters' lives.

But in my quiet, I gave myself the grace to face those deep fears, to face my shadows and dig deeper in to my gratitude. I was thankful for the strength, divine instincts, and protection I had been given by the marriage counselor. When Laerer and I had first met with her, she had the energy of a warm grandmother who was always looking for the good in everyone. She seemed almost humble in her approach. Her soul's mission was to *help* families stay together by using her counseling to *save* the marriage.

She could have kept whatever she knew about Laerer a secret. Instead, she was concerned for my welfare and made it her mission to help me find courage to do the things that were uncomfortable, like facing the truth and stepping into my power.

I was tired of doing all the work, taking care of the kids, financially supporting us, and pretending. The counselor knew the only way to get my attention was to slap me in the face with her words and say, "Wake up! You have got to dig your heels in. You can rest later. You can be passive later. You can feel sorry for yourself later. But now is not the time. Get some courage and fight!"

This was the beginning of my recognition of the power of women. She was a strong woman, and in that moment I needed a strong woman in my corner. My understanding of this kind of divine guidance and the impact that women supporting other women can have in the world came to me out of this terrible experience . . . and I couldn't help but be grateful for that.

When the Student Is Ready, the Teacher Appears

By the time the divorce was final, I lived in a town called Midway, which is about an hour from where I trained my clients in Salt Lake City. I would start each morning by waking up at 4:30 to train my first client, and then be home before my girls got home from school. My roommate was there to help with waking the girls up, making them breakfast, and getting them off to school. In return for helping out with the girls in the mornings and anytime my schedule was crazy, she got free rent since I had a spare room in the basement. It was a win-win for both of us without ever having to exchange money.

Even though I was exhausted, I would buckle up and fill the hour-long drive both ways by doing meditations and visualization exercises and declaring my affirmations. It was me, miles of highway, and my deep willingness to do the work.

I would often grab my phone, as we all do when we are trying to totally numb ourselves from our reality, and pull up inspirational videos on YouTube. That's where I "met" Louise Hay, Deepak Chopra, Jack Canfield, and many others who helped me through my mess. These videos were a free source of wisdom and comfort in a time of desperation.

One morning I discovered a woman named Lisa Nichols. She had a story about how she was broke and didn't even have enough money to buy diapers for her baby. That got my attention!

She was sharing her story of her triumph from being a single mother to becoming a savvy businesswoman, making money by helping the masses through the power of affirmations and owning her soul's call. As I listened to these inspiring people day after day, I felt a glimmer of hope. I started to feel that perhaps my life could be turned around. All these people had gone through so much in their past, yet they had come out on the other end. My soul was telling me I could do the same!

These inspired gurus were all proclaiming the same thing—the power of affirmations, the power of the "word" and seeing and visualizing in your mind where you want to go, and seeing it as if it were already there. I had nowhere to go but up.

Affirmations soon became a regular part of my life, something I would say aloud while I was running, hiking, or driving. Every day I said the following at least 15 times: "Every day I am increasing in success, abundance, and love, and I am inspiring myself, my children, and others to do the same." And because we were nearly destitute in those early days, I'd say, "I am increasing in wealth every day whether I am working, sleeping, or playing. God wants me to be wealthy and stand in my divine rights." They were just words. *But they were so much more than words!* These affirmations would fill my cells with hope.

There's a difference between shoulds versus musts, and affirmations became a must. It wasn't like I thought, I *should* do my affirmations every day. It was instead a need and promise to myself that I would do them, especially on those days I didn't want to, when I was getting in my head about being a terrible mom or thinking I was a financial ruin. I chose to listen to the positive voices of other people until my own voice echoed the same love. The same truth.

One night I sat down and wrote a page and a half—a list of everything that I wanted to create but did not yet believe to be true: I am enough, I am beautiful, I am a financial success, I am a good mom (that was the hardest one), I am making a difference, I am living my dreams—I am, I am, I am, all the way down. Every day I made a commitment that I was going to read and say my affirmations as a "must" because when I was down or angry or depressed—those were the times I needed them the most.

Whenever I felt out of alignment, I would read my affirmations. I would look around my home and feel lonely, depressed, tired, and exhausted, not knowing how to get to my dream but just knowing I needed to get to it. And I would repeat my affirmations.

I needed to inspire my children, showing them a new way as I was showing myself a new way. My dream was stirring inside me, and I knew that despite my current situation, if I didn't express this dream, it would keep me awake at night for the rest of my life. I wanted every woman and man who felt alone—who had lost hope about their health, about their bodies, about their lives—to claim back their truths. I wanted them to ignite their souls so they could live in a body they loved with a life they loved.

I just needed a way to provide for my family as well as fulfill this mission at the same time.

Because there I was, a newly single mom to two beautiful girls who depended on me with their lives. I didn't even have a sheet to fit my old queen-size hand-me-down mattress on the floor, so I used my daughter's extra pink-and-white plaid twin sheet to try to cover my side of the mattress.

Still, I was determined to make a better life for my daughters and myself. I was being buoyed by my dream.

CONVICTION OVER CONVENIENCE

It was in my final rock bottom that I actually had the freedom to Rise. I had no other direction to go but up. I had no mentors to look up to other than my YouTube personas, which made me go within. I sat in my tub. I sat in my bed. I sat in my living room. I sat in my kitchen. I would go within with my affirmations, and something was happening to me. A Divine Feminine awakening was happening in my humbled state of need.

Friends, relationships, money, home, goods, beliefs, and paradigms were all moving out of my life so that I could create new seeds, new ideas, new beliefs. It is in our pain and anguish and downfalls, and in our rock bottom, that we receive the gift to go within so that we can fully Rise.

A few months into single motherhood, I told a few peers that I was looking for a computer, and in no time, I heard of a friend who was throwing away their old computer because it was missing the battery and one of the keys on the keyboard. It was super loud—as in, you could hear the fan humming and echoing through the whole house—and it took about 20 minutes to boot up. If you bumped the computer at all, it turned off immediately and erased anything you'd typed if you hadn't saved it. I was so desperate that I didn't care. As long as the keyboard worked and could stay on if it was plugged in, I wanted it.

I wanted to document and write out all the recipes I was using to transform physically, mentally, and spiritually, as well as what my clients were using to transform. I didn't have Wi-Fi, so thanks to my neighbor who gave me the password, I had free Wi-Fi through our adjoining walls. That dumpy computer was the beginning of the end of my money struggles, and the tool to my success as an entrepreneur. In fact, I created my online programs on that worn-out laptop computer. I used that computer for almost a year because all the money I was making from training was going to feed my girls, pay rent, and pay bills, and any remaining was put toward starting this new business and following my dream.

Every night after I'd put my girls to bed, I'd sit down at my desk, careful not to jostle the computer, and I would write my books, which included *7-Day Jumpstart*, as well as a lot of my early nutrition and recipe website content.

When I closed out the world, the noise, and the TV, I tuned in to my soul. New seeds were being planted, and the idea for my current business was beginning to take shape.

THE DIVINE FEMININE

The year 2012 was incredibly powerful for me. I didn't know it at the time, but I have since learned that all around the world, this same year, women were going through their own struggles and transformations, so that they could get real and raw with their essence, and get to that deep knowing of who they are and what they believe. In fact, it is known in sacred circles as a year of Divine Feminine Rising, a year of magnificent growth through tremendous heartbreak, shattering events, and pain.

That year was my unraveling, my separation, divorce, and heartache, and ended with me hitting a new low yet finding more strength than I ever thought I had. It was the rock bottom that led me on the path of healing my body, my mind, and my spirit—to taking radical ownership for myself, my health, and my life so I could fulfill my purpose in this lifetime.

I had shared my vision with a complete stranger—to help women all over the world. The following year, I started my business thanks to the guidance and support of this kind man, never dreaming he would also become my husband.

I had many reasons to be down on myself, and I certainly entertained playing the victim. I was angry and felt a lack of self-love. But I knew I had two choices—I could either stay at rock bottom, or I could start climbing out. When you feel down on yourself, this is when you *must* declare the truth of your soul. Declare your affirmations. Walk over to your mirror and stand belly to belly with it. Look into your own eyes—really look into them—and make the declarations of your soul.

Say affirmations out loud to yourself, even if the sentences seem forced at first. Speak kind and powerful words over your body, your finances, your family, and your future. As we've already seen, words have the power to transform our lives, our moods, even our DNA. So speak to the Divine Feminine within yourself. She's standing ready for you to rise into your fullest expression of who you are.

THE GAP IN GROWTH

On the way to your dream, you need to know that there will be a gap, a space where it doesn't look rosy. Your dreams will not yet show themselves in the material world. You will be working so hard, but you will not see a single fruit of that labor at that moment. You will be making fine needle-point movements but you won't necessarily see progress—yet.

You have to remember that you've got to do the work. Moving your body, saying your affirmations, eating energizing foods, visualizing, doing some radical truth-telling—these are all powerful tools for transformation.

A lot of people ask me, "How do I stay or get motivated?" But this is the biggest illusion of all. We are all waiting to feel motivated, to feel inspired before we act. The truth is, motivation and inspiration rarely hit you . . . especially if you are in the mud and the muck gasping for air. *You create your momentum.* You have to do the very thing you don't want to do. You have to get into action even when you don't feel like it. Especially if you don't feel like it.

This is the 17-second rule I talk about in my coaching. Basically, when a thought hits, such as *I should work out, I should reach out to this person,* or *I should sign up for that class*—if you don't act on it within 17 seconds, you will talk yourself out of it or you will get distracted with something else. Motivation and inspiration are *not* the sauce for living an epic life. Getting into motion, acting on the hunch, and doing the work, especially when you don't feel like it, are the magic sauce.

What can you start doing daily to create more momentum in your life?

What choice can you make today that will take you one step closer to your dream?

What can you do right now, not 17 seconds from now?

CHAPTER 6

Following the Butterflies

*The cave you fear to enter holds
the treasure you seek.*

— JOSEPH CAMPBELL

The night I found Craig online, I did a keyword search for "fitness" because I wanted to trend in fitness, too. Behind *Oxygen* magazine and two other big brands, number 4 was an actual name, Craig Collins. I dug a little deeper and learned he lived in Vail, Colorado.

When I saw his name on the screen, there was a deep swell of energy inside my belly, almost like a light—a remembrance in my cells was turned on. I knew I needed to reach out to him. I needed to share my dream with him. I found him on Facebook. In my message, I told him I had this amazing dream beating in my heart that I wanted to share with him and see if he could help me.

At the time, Craig was running a social media agency, working with several top food brands, as well as a few celebrities. He just happened to be into fitness and since he knew how to trend in any category, he was trending in fitness. I didn't get a response right away, but I wasn't taking no for an answer, so a few days later I messaged him again.

I knew that social media was the key to sharing information and connecting with a wider audience. I knew also that you could have an amazing product, but if you didn't have marketing, you had nothing—and I didn't know how to market myself or my ideas. As a personal trainer, I knew I could train anybody's body— and that their spirit would come along for the ride. I knew I had a gift for helping other people transform. I needed to share this dream, but I needed help to do it.

Here's the deal: You don't just magically get your dream because you did a lot of "I am" statements in front of your mirror. You grind, you do things that are not convenient, you fight exhaustion late at night, working while others sleep, and then you wake up early to keep at it. You get rejected over and over again—until you don't. So when several days passed with no response from Craig, I wrote to him again . . . and again . . . because at this stage, my vision and dream were bigger than my fears. And I would rather look silly going after my dream than not try at all.

Finally, after about four attempts, Craig responded. He said, "I love helping young entrepreneurs. I would love to help you. When can you jump on a call?"

But I was feeling such an awakening that I thought, *If he is going to be on my team, I need to meet his spirit—in person. I need to make sure he is aligned with my mission and my vision.* I told him I had points to stay at the Marriott so I could drive to Vail and meet him in person.

He probably thought I was crazy, but he agreed to meet me anyway. I offered to take him out to dinner in the hope that he would share his wisdom. Of course he picked the most expensive seafood restaurant, and I was on a tight budget! I did not have money to drop $100 on dinner—but I did it.

He gave off this energy and air of protection and security. I didn't think about it too much at the time, but I remember from that very first meeting how attractive that was. He also had *impeccable* manners. We weren't on a date, obviously, but he behaved like such a gentleman. Not only would he open doors for me, he even unconsciously matched his pace to mine as we walked—little chivalrous gestures I sure was not used to receiving from men.

Over dinner, he graciously shared a lot of marketing knowledge with me, and he was very generous with his time, but it was all going over my head. I didn't have enough of a background to understand everything he was saying or how it applied to me. Then he told me how much he charged, and of course that was not in the cards. So I drove to my hotel after dinner, thinking about everything he'd said. The next day, I thought about him more on my drive home.

I could tell he was heart-centered, but it didn't seem like he was interested in working with me. He hadn't even sounded that excited about my dream. I lost regular contact with him soon after I got back home, and the reality of life kicked in again. We exchanged a few text messages over the next few weeks, but that was about it. What I didn't realize until later was that at that first meeting, something had struck him and something struck me.

Manifestation through Japa Meditation

Fast-forward a few months to a family member's wedding in Hawaii. Since I didn't have a lot of money, I borrowed buddy passes for the flight and decided to camp right on the beach with my daughters in cheap tents with outdoor showers nearby.

It was the best way to connect with Hawaii! My girls were in love with the animals and beautiful exotic plants that surrounded us. They spent nearly every moment barefoot in the sand, on tree swings, and laughing joyfully at the sounds of the ocean and the roosters crowing and running around. For a week, we were part of a little loving community, as we often had dinner with other campers. But the best part was that I could do my Japa meditation on the beach.

During my year of Divine Awakening, I kept up with my affirmations; whenever I was down, I was committed to saying my "I am" affirmations for all the things I wanted to manifest. And anytime I had negative thoughts crowd into my mind, I would *literally drown them out* with the sound of my own voice. I was infusing my brain with massive amounts of positivity.

I'd also begun to dig deep into many meditative techniques and was seeing an incredible amount of growth in my life. I'd discovered Japa meditation through Wayne Dyer's videos on YouTube. With Japa meditation, you take a deep breath in and then make an "Ahhhhhh" sound out of your throat, from your belly, on the exhale. You make that sound as long as the breath will allow, and as you do, you visualize what you are creating. The power of the "Ahhhhhh" sound is the "Ahhhhhh" of God, and the "Ahhhhhh" of orgasm, of creation. This is the sound of life.

Camped out on that beach in Hawaii, I was so excited to do my Japa meditations because I could be as loud as I wanted without anyone hearing me! With my own private beachfront view, I meditated multiple times a day on the sand, surrounded by deep blue water and tropical paradise. The crashing waves covered the sounds I was making for others, but they amplified them for me, allowing me to get into this vortex of a deep, profound meditation.

I visualized my future—what I wanted to create in business *and* in my personal life. I visualized the type of relationship I wanted, the type of man I wanted in my life. I hadn't thought about Craig that much since our dinner meeting, but there on the beach, he popped into my head. That was a little unexpected. But my soul knew. And what I didn't realize was at that very moment, Craig was thinking about me, too.

Six months later, we connected again at an industry event. We sat up late into the night talking, keeping it professional. I learned he was someone who knew what he wanted in life, that he had a lot of integrity. He also had a lot of great ideas around marketing and the use of social media that could help my dream succeed. And then, around midnight, Craig said, "I have to be really honest, because I know you are asking me for business advice, but I am having feelings for you."

Although I was attracted to him on several levels, I had a lot of doubt. My nasty separation had given me a massive distrust of men, and every part of me was on hyper alert. I'd only been with one person, my husband—I didn't know much of anything about dating or what men mean when they say they have "feelings." Did he just mean he wanted to sleep with me?

I insisted we move very, very slowly. In fact, all we did for the next two months was speak on the phone. And even in that distanced kind of connection, Craig built up so much trust in me. If we set a time to speak on the phone, he would *always* call me at precisely that time. He could get hilariously specific about it, too: "I'll call you at 8:20." Not 8:15, not 8:30 . . . 8:20. But he would call on the dot, and I loved how he always *showed up*.

TAKING THE NEXT STEP

Craig and I continued to talk every night the whole time we were dating. And while he offered me so much support, in so many ways, I didn't expect to value his sense of humor so much. You know when someone has your *exact* sense of humor? It's so freeing, and so easy. And while that's certainly important in itself, for me at the time, laughter was something I'd basically forgotten about. I was a single mom! I had no money! I felt like the weight of the world was on my shoulders. Just by making me laugh and reminding me that life was joyful, Craig helped ease that.

We talked about everything—positivity, vision, relationships, our day-to-day routines, and money. It was all so new for me! It was one thing to watch hours of uplifting videos on YouTube, but it was entirely different to have a real person to have these deep discussions with. I was also so attracted to his drive. After my experience with my ex, someone who really had his life together was really appealing! And he inspired me—I believed that I, too, could totally uplevel my life.

After two months of nightly calls, Craig and I decided we should see each other again—by that time, we knew we *really* liked each other! And yet I was so nervous—and not just about whether Craig would break my heart (although that fear was definitely there!), but also what Craig would think of me and my life. I still wasn't making much money, and our house was *empty*. We laugh about it still, but Craig started dating me when I had a mattress on the floor and tinfoil on my TV. I'm sure the moment he walked in the door, he thought, *Holy crap, this girl is not doing well.*

That is when the truth about my divorce and my life came out. You can hide your truth and pain behind a kind smile, but you can't hide the fact that you are sleeping on a mattress on the floor and don't even have the correct size sheet to cover it.

Samantha was three that first time Craig came to visit. She was very shy and reluctant to bond with anyone outside of me and her sister. It was hard to even get her to engage or sit on grandparents' laps. I had been so anxious about introducing my children to this man who was rapidly becoming important to me. Would they get along? I knew I could count on Sarah to be warm and polite (and then give me her opinion later!). But Samantha was just so very shy. I warned Craig that she probably wouldn't even look at him for the entire visit.

But Craig had that calm, grounding presence. After I made the introductions, Craig took a seat in the chair in the living room. Samantha was quietly playing with her dolls on the floor when I went to the bathroom, and when I came out, I couldn't believe my eyes. She had crawled onto Craig's lap with her blanket and was leaning against him watching TV. She *never* did that. I was dumbfounded, but also completely melting inside. This little angel was a good judge of character, and her trust in him gave me the strength to trust him, too.

Soon after Craig visited me for the first time, he started sending me random checks and cash in the mail. Or he would send money with a specific note like: "Go to the movies." I'd finally told him about the money being taken from our bank accounts, and while he wasn't offering to pay my bills for me, nor would have I expected him to or accepted it if he had, every month that he chose to send me a gift was another opportunity for him to express his affection and care for me. It was another opportunity for me to learn to trust and be thankful that he believed in me and was impressed that I was hustling to make a better life for myself and my girls.

TRUSTING MY BODY

My marriage to my ex was not a positive one in many ways—including in the bedroom. Despite getting pregnant three times, Laerer and I weren't intimate all that often, partly because we weren't emotionally intimate and also because I found sex physically painful. It certainly wasn't pleasurable.

So, when I worked up the courage to connect physically with Craig for the first time, I experienced a breakthrough. I had thought sex just wasn't for me! I thought there was something *wrong* with my body. But the first time we had sex, I had an *orgasm.* There was no pain!

Obviously, that experience was great for a lot of reasons, but it taught me something I had never truly understood: My body *knows.*

Our bodies are constantly speaking to us, and they never lie! If something doesn't feel right *in your body*, then it isn't right. That moment, when I went from painful to ecstatic sex, allowed me to trust the messages I receive from my body.

A Partnership for Mindful Health

Here's the thing about Craig: He never rushes into *anything*. He's an extremely mindful person, and he meditates every day. Honestly, one of our early dates was *three days of meditation*. When I went to his house for the first time, I saw a huge shelf full of self-development books and books on meditation—things that I was just getting into. I really respected what I saw. I understand now why he was so willing to move at my slow, sacred pace—he truly lives life with intention.

So when we started talking about starting a new business, we approached the subject thoughtfully and mindfully. But we were excited! And we had a *ton* of ideas. I was so excited about this potential opportunity and was eager to share this news with someone whose opinion I respected—my father. As perhaps I should have expected, he had his doubts and was not afraid to share them with me.

With the sting of my divorce and recent financial ruin still lingering, my father was not thrilled about my feelings for Craig or my ideas for a business. First he told me I was never going to be able to do an online business and that I should just stick with training. Then he said I'd lose all my money and it wasn't going to work out. He said he'd seen people fail time and time again. My dad's fears about money, success, and following your dreams wanted to take root in my own mind.

People get great ideas to start businesses all the time, but then as soon as they share their dream, other people tell them they're going to fail and that it's not the safe and responsible thing to do. But my dream was so big in my heart that I was willing to step into that fear, invest the little money I had, and hand over 50 percent of the business to someone I was just getting to know. I was willing to work on it late at night when the kids were asleep. It was a huge moment of following the butterflies. Yes, it was scary. And yes, I really did have to consider the possibility that it could fail horribly and I would have to stick with personal training. You know what? I did it anyway, even though I didn't feel supported by family or have a group of investors. It was just me and Craig against the world. I found myself in the familiar position of being unsupported in my decision. The last time I felt this way, I made it to the top 10. But this time, I had a partner beside me. Together, I truly believed we could accomplish the unthinkable. And if we never tried, we would never know.

A client, who was an attorney, was willing to help me out and was ruthless with me and made sure we did our due diligence. He insisted that Craig and I write up a contract together and that we really look at things from a business standpoint when it came to partnering together, trying not to let our emotions cloud the issue. It was a risk for both of us. Craig put all his money into growing this business—my dream—not knowing for sure if it would pan out, but trusting that it would. And it did!

We were the perfect pair. The yin and the yang. I held the vision, I shared my message, and Craig made sure that my message was heard. Together, we were committed to transforming the world. And now Craig is the CEO and manages a team of 58 full-time employees. Our e-mail list goes out to 1.5 million active recipients a day. We have 1.3 million active Facebook followers. We get around 600,000 to 800,000 views on each live video we post. And we have reached 90 million households around the globe within six months with our live videos.

But it wasn't always sunshine and roses.

I had survived being a single mom, working multiple jobs, and was creating books late at night that I was going to be able to market and sell. I *thought* that I knew what it meant to be busy. Then we started this business together, and I worked so much harder and longer than I had ever worked in my life. I was still getting up at 4:30 A.M. and working my training job. I was still creating programs and trying to provide customer service and be the creator of content and creator of videos, while Craig was trying to do all the marketing pieces. It took some time to iron out our strengths and weaknesses, as well as our individual roles, as a business partnership. But we used all our tools of empathy and communication, and our vision and positivity, and we grew into our roles and into one another.

An Unexpected Love

Craig stepped into my life as a partner and into the lives of my daughters as a caretaker. He is there for them as a strong, safe father, providing all the necessities of life. And the best part is that when we parent together, we have so much fun doing it! Eventually, we decided to make an even deeper commitment. We decided to get married.

But as the wedding date drew closer, the doubts let themselves in unannounced. Craig was wonderful and kind and was an amazing partner, but would he stab me in the back? Would he take my money, cheat on me, or fall out of love with me? Would he hurt me like I'd been hurt before? My ex was the father of my children, had my back when he thought I loved him, and then literally tried to take me under when I removed my love, so in my mind, everything was a possibility.

These were real concerns, and as a single mom, I had to make sure that I would be okay if the worst happened. So I checked in with my fears.

Would I still have a place to live if this relationship didn't work out? *Yes.*

Could I still make a good living as a trainer if my business idea didn't take off? *Yes.*

Could I still provide for my daughters as a single mom? *Yes. Proved that one already in spades.*

How would I feel if he weren't a part of my life or the girls' lives? *I would feel such a huge loss.*

My head was saying, *He could hurt you. He could take advantage of you. He could leave you.* But my heart was telling me, *He loves you dearly. Trust that. He will help you achieve your dreams. He is a man of integrity.*

Rising is a journey, a daily practice. And just because things start to look up, it doesn't mean that you are all of a sudden 100 percent healed and enlightened. It doesn't mean that old fears won't come knocking on your door at night or that your ego will stop speaking to you. But we get to choose to follow the pull of the Universe. We get to take a risk. We get to follow those butterflies and dive headfirst into love, without the 100 percent money-back guarantee.

THE WEDDING

At the base of the Maroon Bells Mountains in Aspen, Colorado, I was gathered with my girls, ready to walk down the aisle, surrounded by our close friends and family. With majestic mountains as a backdrop, wildflowers of every color, and the bright blue sky, it was a picture-perfect backdrop for the small, intimate wedding.

My daughters were my flower girls, and seeing them so excited and happy made my heart sing. I was wearing a borrowed sleeveless dress that my best friend's mother loaned me. It fit me like a glove and I felt so beautiful in it. As I was walking down the aisle, I was trying to take in everything—the beautiful view around me, the fact that I was actually getting married again, that my daughters were getting a responsible and loving bonus dad, and that I was surrounded by my friends and family I loved.

But I was walking by myself, unsupported by the man who was supposed to give me away. My father had told me that he wouldn't walk me down the aisle because I was wearing a sleeveless dress. He felt that was inappropriate, but I suspected the reasons went deeper than a dress. Maybe he was ashamed of the person I was marrying. Maybe he was ashamed that I wasn't getting married to someone from the church. In any case, while he was certainly there, my father felt it was best that he sit instead. So I stopped midway down the aisle, and then Craig, so chivalrous and understanding, walked to get me and walked me the rest of the way.

It was beautiful but it was different, and that was okay. I was making a declaration in that moment to be happy, despite my awareness that my parents were not supportive of this marriage.

Right after we got married, we had a luncheon, and my parents took off before it began—but not before my dad shared with me that most people that get divorced will get divorced again. He had no hope for us as a couple and probably very little left in me as a person. Here was their daughter, not going to church anymore, marrying a nonmember of the church, and wearing a sleeveless dress. I think they were terrified. So while my parents were very cordial when they were there, they did the bare minimum to be able to say they participated in some way.

I wish that I hadn't allowed it to affect me, but it did. It felt like they were showing me that my decisions, my dreams, and my choices were not approved by them, and therefore not important.

SETTING BOUNDARIES WITH FAMILY

The truth is that my parents had barely been in the same room with Craig before the wedding. They were understandably scared of my new relationship (well, so was I!), but they let their fear prevent them from getting to know him. At first they refused to even *meet* him, and for the longest time they wouldn't come over if he was there. But Craig never came down on them. His attitude toward my parents (and toward my ex, who I was almost constantly angry at) was and is "They are in a lot of pain. Just send love." That could get frustrating, to be honest! Sometimes, I just wanted to vent! But Craig always tried to see the best in people and respond with his own best in return.

But it wasn't just my parents' attitude toward Craig that hurt. Each verbal jab would create negative vibrations in my body. I could be flying high, but their words could bring me down in an instant.

Craig helped me find a solution. While never once being critical of my parents, he encouraged me to set boundaries. He had been watching my responses to my parents, and was hurting with me on my behalf. He reminded me of something I was constantly forgetting: that I get to decide how people treat me.

He was pretty ruthless with me! He said that until I show them how they can treat me, it is my own fault they are treating me this way. And he was right. I realized if I wanted to go to the next level, I needed to get adamant, too—about who I allowed in my space, the conversations, the experiences. I could continue going through the motions, listening to my parents tell me negative things every time they called and make passive-aggressive comments that brought me down, or I could set a very clear boundary that I was not going to tolerate those types of conversations, those jabs and stabs.

So I wrote a lengthy letter to my parents telling them how much I appreciated them, loved them, and understood that they were doing the best with what they knew, but I was an adult, and I was doing the best I could, too. I was no longer going to accept any negativity about my lifestyle, my decisions, how I was raising my kids, who I married, or whether I practiced religion or not. Even if it was in a phone call or a visit, I would end the conversation and remove myself from it. I said they had a choice—they could choose to be in my life and accept the choices I made and keep their opinions to themselves. Or they could choose to remove themselves from my life. I was done with letting them bully me. I was done with letting them tell me I wasn't a good mom because I wasn't taking my kids to church. It was throwing me into a spiral after every phone call. It was a very difficult conversation, but I knew I had to do it. I prepared myself to accept the consequences.

It was a very difficult letter to write. I broke down in tears a few times as I struggled to say what I *needed* to say, knowing that I had to hold my ground, but terrified of what their reaction might be. I had been practicing being my own best friend and teaching people how to treat me, but my parents were the people I loved the most. I didn't know how they'd receive it or if they would even want to have me in their lives, but I needed to say *my truth*.

For many months after the wedding, my parents and I didn't speak much. My mom would call and want to talk about religion or about how I was parenting my girls and not bringing them to church. I would kindly remind her that those discussions were no longer allowed and to not bring those topics up again. Other times I had to politely hang up the phone when they kept talking about those topics, even after I'd asked them to stop.

I know that caused a lot of heartache for my mom, because she felt like she had lost her daughter. It wasn't an easy time for me, either. But with Craig's support, I was able to maintain those boundaries in a space of love, so that when I felt their pushback, I didn't feel like I had lost them.

It took about six months for them to finally accept that I was serious, and after that, we were able to have normal and enjoyable conversations without any negativity. This last piece of really loving myself was the hardest piece, because I loved my family. I had let them do and say what they wanted to in a lot of ways because I had such loyalty. Standing up for myself was uncomfortable, but necessary. And you know what? Now they absolutely *adore* Craig. We are so much closer for having gone through this honest and open reset of boundaries.

People will treat you the way you allow them to treat you, and people will shift when you show up for yourself. The more you love yourself, the stronger you will reflect love. And one beautiful way you can show love to yourself and to others is through the power of words.

The Power of Words

I came out of my year of Divine Awakening knowing that I needed to fully embrace a new energy in my life. I was waking up at warp speed. And since I saw such great results in my own life from these new practices, I wanted to introduce my daughters to them in a way they'd understand. One of the easiest ways was through the power of words and molecules.

I'd heard about a researcher and healer in Japan, Dr. Masaru Emoto, who studied molecules of water and the impact both positive and negative thoughts had on the molecules. It was such a fascinating concept that I decided to do an experiment with my daughters. We took grains of rice and placed them in three separate jars. We put a sign that said "positive" on the outside of one of the jars. On the second jar, we wrote a minus sign and "negative." With the third jar, we wrote "ignore." We placed them in the same spot in our home, where they were getting the same light and temperature.

Each day, we would walk by the jar that said "negative," and we would say mean words to the rice— words like, "I hate you. You are ugly. You are dumb." The one that said, "ignore," we wouldn't give any attention at all. Then, for the third one, we would say loving words to the jar, such as "I love you. You are beautiful. I love having you around."

I had no idea whether it would work, but my daughters were benefiting from the experiment anyway—it felt horrible to say those awful things to the grains of rice! They didn't deserve it. It was a powerful lesson in empathy.

And then, after about two weeks, we noticed that the rice that we had said negative things to had gotten all moldy and rotten. The rice that was being ignored had started to go bad, too. And when we looked at the jar with the positive sign—nothing was wrong with it! My daughters were astonished—and even though I already knew the power of words, I was, too.

Our body is over 70 percent water. The words we speak and the energy we carry can shift the molecular structure of our cells, either for the positive or for the negative. We know this on a scientific level. Every time I am about to drink water, I say an affirmation such as, "I love myself. I trust myself. I trust in the process of life. I am safe." And then I drink it. That positive energy is directed to the water, and into the water in your body.

FACING YOUR FEAR

We are one decision away from being in a better relationship, being a better parent, starting a new career, or speaking our truth. The problem is that we are waiting to *feel* like acting on those decisions, and the truth is we may never get there. We may never *feel* like this is the right time. Instead of waiting for all the stars to align and for that "perfect moment," we can choose to face our fears head on, choose to follow the butterflies and see where they take us.

Fear is a very real emotion and we all experience it. You can probably list several fears you have right now in your relationships, in your career, or in your life. Fear can *rob* you of the amazing experiences in life. We are not designed to go after the things in life that are scary, out of our comfort zone, or difficult, but if we stand eye to eye with fear, we can really look at it—and see that it is just an invitation to take a step further.

Whether it's a fluttering in your belly, a stiffness in your shoulders, or a stirring or an uneasiness you can't quite describe, it sends a signal to the brain to be on alert.

Maybe you get great ideas when you are in the shower or bath, or even before bed, and you think of something you never thought of before and it gets you excited. You know it came from someplace different, someplace special. When inspiration hits you, remember that you have about 17 seconds to write it down or act upon it before your brain will try to talk you out of it and create all these signals that make you super uncomfortable. Soon enough you will be saying, "Wow, I was crazy for thinking that. Forget that idea!"

For some of you out there, your brain will trick you through procrastination. You might have the best idea for a business pop into your head, but instead of taking action and grabbing a notepad and a pen, you find yourself saying, "I am just too busy," as you scroll mindlessly through Facebook for an hour. Be honest with yourself and take a look at where fear is showing up in your life. Where are you allowing fear to be in the driver's seat of your life? Don't let something as powerless as fear keep you from your soul's call. Instead, allow fear to be your indicator that something wonderful is just around the corner.

When I sense a stirring and my body tenses, I ask myself, *Will this hurt me? Will anyone get hurt if I implement this idea?* And if the answer is no, which it most always is, then I realize the fear is false; it's made up. Fear will be with you always, and instead of running from it, you should thank it. Thank it for keeping you safe. Thank it for showing up in your body, indicating to your cells your best next move. We need to learn to step in, grab the steering wheel, and drive, even with fear in the passenger's seat.

Beyond the fear and the butterflies is the oasis—the dream, the awakening, the manifestation of all the things you're creating and wanting in your life. You are going to have to do those things that scare you. Don't wait for motivation because that may or may not come (usually it doesn't). Instead, say, "Thanks, fear. I got this!" And get curious about where the butterflies are leading you—stay in that curiosity and take action! The more you move in action and see the amazing horizons that you can reach, the more you build confidence in yourself and in your Rise.

Where are the feelings of fear showing up in your life?

How can you view those fears as invitations?

Where in your life do you need to set boundaries and become your own best friend?

CHAPTER 7

The Universal Law of Forgiveness

The practice of forgiveness is our most important contribution to the healing of the world.

— Marianne Williamson

Despite all my growth and all my happiness with Craig, the anger was still strangling me. I could feel it in every part of my body. One minute I could be watching my daughters run around, and the next, I would find my mind flashing back to past wounds from my ex. Anger would unexpectedly surge through me, stealing my enjoyment of the sweet moments of life. I hadn't fully forgiven Laerer or myself, and that lack of forgiveness was poisoning me.

I wanted to release myself from the bonds of guilt. Guilt for putting my kids through divorce. Guilt for not listening to my intuition on my wedding day. Guilt for numbing out for so many years. And I wanted to release my ex and his wrongdoings from my thoughts. I wanted to walk my future path with hope, a lightness to my step, and a deep love for myself through forgiveness that I knew my kids would sense.

I *wanted* all these things, but all I *felt* was anger and guilt.

And so, seven months after Craig and I got married, we decided to move to Costa Rica as a family for three months. I had been to Costa Rica on retreats and with clients, so I knew it was a place that could be profoundly healing for my family. We needed to take the time to unite and create a new way of being as a family and as individuals.

The rawness of nature shook up our daily patterns and lifestyle to help us create what we truly wanted, clearing us out and making us new. It was a wild and beautiful time. And for me, it was necessary in my journey to forgiveness.

About a month into our time in Costa Rica, a medicine woman told me about an upcoming ceremony that would be led by a Colombian healer. I'd read about a vine that has been used for more than 5,000 years by the healers of the Amazon as a way to reconnect with yourself, find forgiveness, remove addictions, and help make important decisions. I had never tried any substances at this point in my life, but I knew I needed to do this because I was still resentful with myself and with my ex.

The ceremony using this plant was to be held on the exact date I got married to my ex-husband. As the day drew near, I ate specific healing foods, and fasted the day before and the day of the ceremony. I prepared my mind and body for what I hoped would be a life-changing experience.

This beautiful feminine plant could teach me a very important lesson—a lesson in trust and staying in love and forgiveness. I was told that if your intention is pure, she'll always show up and show you what you need to see. This plant is loving, but fierce. She is the mother who disciplines you when you need correcting, and holds you in tender embrace when you need extra love and safety. And she does it in her way, with her timing— not yours.

I sat in the ceremony with the shaman all night long. He wore colorful clothing and a feathered headdress as he sang, danced, and called on higher powers. I didn't experience vomiting or diarrhea, nor any of the visions that people around me were having. I was trying to figure out why nothing was happening. *I set my intention. It has to be coming, right? I want to be talked to. I want to be shown.*

Several hours into the experience, the shaman called me up. With a smile spread across his wrinkled, weathered face, he indicated through the translator that he wanted me to take even more of the medicine, which tasted like sludge or very pungent earth. And I had already been taking more than anyone else.

He started tapping on my heart and my head as the translator told me what he was saying. I had to be willing to open my heart and quit shutting everything out. I instantly felt a little defensive, although I didn't respond. I was thinking, *I am! I do! I'm kind and loving. I'm here because I want to open my heart!* Over and over, the shaman kept saying, "It's closed," as he tapped on my head and heart, trying to open my highest chakras to get the energy flowing. I eventually went back to my seat. But I never felt a single sensation.

When the morning light peeked through the trees, the other participants started to pack up their things to go. I was still lying there on my mat with the worst feeling in my heart, because now everyone was starting to chitchat and talk about their experiences with the medicine. And I had felt *nothing.* I was in such a space of self-pity, because I felt I'd done everything *right.* The shaman had called me up to do work on me specifically. I drank more than anyone else! Why didn't I have an experience?

We walked to the house to have breakfast and people began openly sharing their beautiful moments in greater detail. I had nothing to share, so I sat in silence, wondering if I was ever going to receive the answers I was seeking. Maybe I really was broken.

Leaving that space after breakfast, I decided to walk down to the beach. I took a winding path through overgrown trees and tropical greenery, and on that path I decided to surrender. *I give up. I'm trying to be a better person . . . but I give up. I stayed up all night and drank the plant medicine, and I'm done trying.*

I was almost to the beach when my feet felt even more connected to the earth. I felt the softness of the dirt path, the plants brushing my legs. I spread my towel on the private beach and laid down for a nap.

As soon as I closed my eyes, I felt as if my body was being scanned from above in a peaceful and beautiful way, and I could see it all happening as if I were hovering above myself. The scan stopped at my belly, where I could only see black. The wave of energy then continued over and over until my belly turned a beautiful red. And from where it was the most vibrant in the center, a beautiful vine started to grow.

As the vine—this plant medicine—started to grow inside me, she spoke ancient wisdom: "I am you, and you are me. All the beauty you see around the world, all the beauty that you aspire to, *you are that.*" A tropical pink flower began to grow on the vine and her words came again, "You are just as beautiful as that flower." My mind flashed to a scene where I was sitting next to a girl I didn't know, and I was judging her. In my mind, I had said some not-so-nice things about her.

When I saw myself sitting next to this girl, judging her, my neck muscles began to tighten. The pain grew, cramping to the point that it was concerning me, even in my visionary state. I opened my eyes to look around the beach when the voice spoke again: "You know that pain you feel in your neck? That's from you not loving as hard as you can love. Not reaching out to people you see every day—ignoring the lady on the bus so you don't have to talk to a stranger. The woman with the hysterical kid in the grocery store, the one you're judging—that's your pain. Your judgment is your pain. As soon as you can let go of judgment and offer up love and see them as the souls they are, your pain will be freed."

I closed my eyes and began to reflect on all the people I had judged and the little judgments I made each day. I pictured each person I'd ever felt annoyed by, and I said, "I'm sorry. I see you." With those words, the pain in my neck began to ease a little.

Then I saw my ex-husband. In my vision, I was able to feel his presence next to me and look him deep in the eyes. I looked into his soul and said, "I'm so sorry for not seeing you as the human you are, and the soul you are. I forgive you." My neck started to loosen a little bit more.

Another face moved into my vision. It was me—my long hair, my blue eyes, my hidden fears. My dreams. My hope. I looked myself in the eyes, and with unconditional love and with the deepest emotion I could muster, I said, "I forgive you. I love you. You're doing the best you can with what you have. I trust you." With those words, my neck was completely free of pain. I continued lying there, thankful for this beautiful moment, and feeling so free, so light, and more connected to something bigger than I've ever felt before.

As I slowly opened my eyes minutes later, I saw seagulls of freedom and forgiveness flying all around me.

It Doesn't Happen Overnight

After that amazing experience in Costa Rica, I thought I had forgiven my ex-husband completely. I tried to honor that forgiveness, but it was difficult, because it wasn't like our relationship changed overnight. Laerer was still doing all the same things that would make my gut wrench. Craig reminded me that we could either let my ex take control of our emotions or send him love, because he was obviously in pain. So we would close our eyes—sometimes mine were clenched in frustration—and send him love. The first few times, it was difficult, but it got easier. Even if I started in anger, I would take a deep breath and then think: *Wherever you are, I hope you feel good and I hope you are surrounded in light.*

I did this every day, and every time something wasn't going according to schedule.

But I realized that every time I saw Laerer in person, I was still unable to look him in the eye, let alone hug or touch him. I knew that meant there was still work to be done. I knew this was my opportunity.

Back home in the serenity of my bedroom, I started with mirror work. I needed to focus on my own forgiveness first. I needed to forgive the little girl who was in pain, who felt unloved, and who believed she was not enough. I wanted a different reality now.

I would stand in front of the mirror and look myself in the eyes and cry and say, "I forgive you. I love you."

Then I'd say, "I forgive myself. I love myself. I'm sorry."
And I'd list specific things I remembered doing or saying
that were damaging to my soul.

I also wrote down exactly what I wanted to happen in
detail—how I saw my relationship with Laerer and how I
dreamed it would be, even if that seemed near impossible.
Then I started looking at the specific things he did that
hurt me, and asked myself, "Where have I hurt him?" I
began to realize that I'd hurt him so much in things I had
said and leaving him when I'd let him believe that I was
going to stay with him. I finally understood that I was no
different than he was.

This is deep shadow work. It is *hard*. And it has to be
done every single day.

When I would do my daily visualization work,
focusing on what I wanted in my reality, I would include
Laerer. I would visualize him receiving love, and I would
visualize the two of us operating in a space of forgiveness,
co-parenting in kindness.

This was not easy! I would get enraged *all the time*.
Every time he didn't pay child support or didn't support
the girls, I wanted to respond in anger, but I refused to
allow myself to do so. I would feel my emotions, I would
recognize and allow them, and then I would remind
myself that Laerer was hurting. I responded with *kindness*
and made the choice to send him love instead.

I believed Laerer and I would one day be friends. We
would forgive the pain we had inflicted on each other.
We would be able to look into each other's eyes. And we
would try to help one another be better parents.

Up until this point—almost two years after my
experience with the plant medicine in Costa Rica—
Laerer had never been allowed in my home. My home

was my sanctuary. But Sarah, my oldest, was going to her first homecoming dance, and all her friends were going to come to the house for dinner and take pictures before going off to the dance. This was a huge deal for us—as powerful as her first steps as a baby.

I knew that I needed to be in radical kindness, that I needed to invite Laerer to be present for that experience. Now, that did *not* feel good—despite all this work, I still had a lot of negative energy attached to Laerer. But I had learned to trust the inspirations that came with my visualizations.

I called him to invite him, and then I took it a step further. He lived in a different state, and I offered to pay for his flight and his hotel room so that he could be there to share this moment with us. He had dinner with us, watched Sarah with her friends alongside of us, took pictures of her, and saw her receive her flower from her date and then go off to the very first dance of her lifetime.

Two days after that experience, I got a note from him. It was the first note of kindness I had received from him in the six years since our separation. He thanked me for all of it—for the flight and the hotel room, and for welcoming him into my home and our lives.

That letter meant a lot, of course, but it was my willingness to get radically kind and to do what my soul was asking me to do that created a healing for me. My own actions changed our experience.

And three weeks later, I had a breakthrough. I had dropped off the girls to visit Laerer, and I discovered that I was able to look him in the eye, without judgment, for the very first time. I found myself spontaneously hugging him good-bye. When I got into the car where Craig was waiting, I shook my head in disbelief. I said, "I cannot believe I just hugged him and it didn't feel weird. I don't feel weird. I feel good!"

It took a long time, but I was able to transition from rage every time I saw him to slowly getting better and better, to now being able to have a conversation with normal eye contact and give him a good-bye hug. In fact, ever since then, our exchanges have been very amicable and stress-free.

Soon enough, I'd find myself in another situation in need of forgiveness, and it all started with a phone call.

STUBBORN AS A MULE

"Hello?"

"Danette . . . I don't think your dad is going to make it," my mom replied.

Early that morning, my 73-year-old dad had been riding his mule with my brothers in the backcountry when he was kicked off. Speculation was that the stubborn mule didn't like the uncomfortable handmade saddle my dad was using, and he bucked, sending my dad onto the jagged rocks that littered the mountains. Dad landed on his spine and was unresponsive, not moving at all.

My brothers were scared to death to move him, but they managed to get him to a hospital. That's when Mom had called me in massive panic. After many tests, it was clear that he'd broken his hip, his clavicle, his shoulder, and injured his spine. Results were inconclusive, but if his life was spared, odds were he was going to be a paraplegic. That was the best-case scenario.

There was not much I could do but pray and meditate, send them all love, and try to keep my mother calm on the phone. My brothers kept calling me periodically, saying my dad was stable, in a brace, and couldn't move. They finally said he was not going to die, but they didn't think he'd be able to walk again.

Three months before my dad's accident, I'd had a breakdown moment.

When my husband had asked what was wrong, I had said, "Craig, my parents are getting old and they could die, and I don't want my dad to die without asking for forgiveness, leaving this world with words he couldn't take back. Leaving without reconciliation and the love I knew was available to us." I didn't want to repeat the karma or feel any bad energy with either of my parents. "This has to be cleared, and I don't know how to clear it."

At this point, we were still going through our period of setting boundaries, and there was a lot of resentment and hurt circling around the relationship. I decided I would visit them that summer and tell them how I felt, hoping we could clear all hurtful energy—but my dad's accident happened before I could get up there.

After 10 days, my dad came home from the hospital. He was not a paraplegic, but he was in a full-body brace and needed around-the-clock assistance. Mom had to help him take his pants off and on, sit him down, lay him down, and help him use the restroom. While there were other people there to help, it was too much stress on her system. On his very first night home, I got the call that my mom had been admitted to the hospital with breathing issues. Her organs were shutting down and she wasn't in great health to begin with.

I called my dad immediately. "I am coming up and I am going to take care of you. Don't tell mom. I am going to surprise her and see her in the hospital." My dad is not an emotional man, but he started sobbing on the phone. Through the tears, I heard him say, "That would mean a lot!"

I flew back home that night. When I walked into my mom's hospital room, she was so drugged up she thought she was dreaming when she saw me, but I wanted to say hello before I went to the house to see my dad. I knew they were both scared, and so was I. It was total chaos, but at the same time, it was the best gift ever for our family.

I went to the house in the middle of the night, just in time to help give my dad his pain medication. Once I saw how much help both my parents needed, I decided to stay there and take care of my dad for the next five days until my mom got out of the hospital.

My dad didn't make it easy. He has a super-strong will, and I think I am very much like him. We are very opinionated. We speak our minds. It can cut people and it can hurt people. He has certainly cut me and hurt me— but I respect him for his honesty. He always speaks his mind and you always know what he is thinking.

He was also a rule follower. My whole upbringing was built around the idea that my parents did all the right things. They went to church every Sunday. They didn't question their faith, their marriage, or their way of life. Nevertheless, I would soon learn that this was another way my dad and I were alike: He liked to bend the rules a bit, even when it went against doctor's orders.

The second day there, I found myself looking for him around the house. I had only left him alone for 20 minutes. He had a full back brace on, could barely walk, was taking every medicine imaginable to man, and was using a walker to get to the bathroom and back to his rocking chair, where he would sleep and sit all day so his back could heal.

Had he fallen, passed out, hit his head? I checked every bedroom and still could not find him. Then I looked outside and saw that the car was missing. My dad had *taken the car*! Obviously he was strictly forbidden to drive. He could barely move! If he hit his head or God forbid crashed into another driver, he could die. And I was the one who was supposed to be making sure Dad didn't do anything stupid!

Now I wasn't just panicked, I was angry. Where could he have gone? I called my brothers, and within minutes, the whole family was in *go mode* because we knew the gravity of the situation.

My soul is always talking, and mine told me to look over at the neighbors' house by Dad's garden. Sure enough, I got a glimpse of him standing by his car. I ran through the field as fast as I could sprint. As I caught up to him and gasped for air, my phone rang. It was my brother. He wanted to know if I had found dad.

I looked into my dad's eyes and I saw something different. He was pleading for me to not rat him out, to have his back, to understand. Everything inside of me wanted to yell at my father and call in the family so we could all yell at him together, but instead I quickly and calmly told my brother that all was well.

"Dad, get in the car." I knew I didn't need to ream him out for what he was doing and say how disappointed I was in him. Instead, I needed to love him, to see him, to give him exactly what I had wanted all along growing up—grace.

Suddenly my sister-in-law's car appeared at the end of the driveway, ready to pull in. Even from 15 feet away, I could see she was enraged and about to let my dad have it for doing something that could jeopardize his health.

I looked over at my dad with a sly smile and said, "Let's get out of here."

He smiled back like we were teenagers in trouble together, caught by our shenanigans. He laughed and said, "Floor it!" I peeled out, leaving my sister-in-law in the dust. As we headed out on the road, we started laughing hard. We knew we were breaking the rules. It felt damn good to break the rules.

But the next time Dad ignored doctor's orders and broke the rules, I wasn't so nice. And that's exactly what he needed.

Two days later, I woke up to noise at 5:30 in the morning—Dad was dragging the very full garbage bag from the kitchen out to the garage! I jumped out of bed and started yelling at him before I even made it out of the house.

"What are you doing!?"

He said, "Well, the trash needs to go out today."

In a very terse voice, I told him I was going to take care of the trash and he was going to ruin everything and not be able to walk again if he didn't listen to the doctor's orders. This was the first time I'd ever yelled at my dad.

"You really care about me," he said, looking a little surprised.

"Yes!" I shouted. "People actually care about you! I want you around! Don't mess this up!"

He started to cry as I helped him back into the house. Then I realized that in his mind, my getting mad at him and yelling at him was a form of caring about him. This was how he'd treated me my whole life—getting mad at me, holding me to a high standard—and to him, it was his way of showing me he cared about me. I'm not saying it was the right way to do it—I certainly never felt like I ever lived up to any of his expectations. But here, with my dad in a back brace, I could start to look at a lot of those interactions under a different light.

Later that afternoon, I got him into the car again for his next doctor's appointment. The doctor checked his back brace, and everything looked fine. Again, I didn't bother to mention my dad was taking out the trash earlier that day.

Dad's tone had softened immensely since my yelling fit. And on our car ride home, as I carefully drove the winding back roads to our house, he started the conversation that put us on a new path.

"There is a quote that says you can't erase the past, but you can create a new ending." Dad paused for a moment, and he took a deep breath. "I am really hoping I can do that with you and Craig." He turned to me, and he had tears streaming down his face. "I have really messed up. I am really sorry for hurting you and not supporting you, and I can see that you are married to a great guy who loves those girls and loves you"

My dad had just unloaded layers of sadness and guilt and was asking for forgiveness from his little girl, his grown daughter. *Why are you not crying? Your dad is sobbing. This is everything you have ever wanted to hear.* I had wanted this conversation for months—years, even. But in the moment, I had no idea what to say.

I felt years of anger, disappointment, and feeling misunderstood start to slide out of my body, through my seat, and onto the road as we turned the corner into the driveway, to our new relationship built on love and mutual respect.

There were a million things I could have said. But in the end, all I said was, "Thanks, Dad. That means a lot. I forgive you."

It meant everything.

THE PATH TO FREEDOM

Forgiveness is the greatest act of self-love we can give ourselves. It is essential to our Rise. It doesn't mean we accept the wrongs done to us. It means we free ourselves from hate. From anger. From low vibrations. If someone does not fully forgive themselves and those who have offended them, they will carry an energetic cord and continue to attract circumstances, people, and events in their lives (including stress-related illnesses) that will reflect that pain or wound. When we are free from the heaviness of hatred, our souls—now light and at peace—can continue to lift us higher and higher on the Rise to our true selves.

Some people are mad at God for taking their kids away. Others are seething at family members who sexually assaulted them. I know women and men who cannot let go of the pain and deceit and anger from when their spouse cheated on them. Listen to me—you have every reason to feel anger in these situations! I am in no way saying that your anger is wrong or unwarranted. What I am saying is that if it is left unaddressed, it can hold you back from living a full, embodied life of happiness. It keeps you living with your intense pain, and that is a tragedy.

Forgiveness is not about righting the wrong. It's not about forgetting. It's not about covering it up, burying it, or sprinkling confetti on it so you can just get on with your life already. Forgiveness is about freeing yourself from the low vibrations, thoughts, and energies that your mind is creating.

A few months ago, I was doing one-on-one coaching with a beautiful woman whom I'll call Molly who had put on 40 pounds of extra weight over the past 20 years. If you were to glance at her, you would see a woman who seemed to have it pretty good. She had a home, held a steady job, and made a decent income. She always did her hair and had plenty of new high-end clothes. She and her husband had been married for about 10 years, and he also had a good job.

But if you looked deep within, if you were to ask for her stories, you would find a great deal of pain. She was sexually abused by her brother when she was 14. Every day, something would remind her of her brother, and in a flash she would remember the horrific images of what he did to her. She would feel the tension in her gut and shoulders, and she would want to run away, but then she'd realize she was sitting in front of her desk at work. She would stare at her screen, and with her fingers pounding harder on the keyboard, she would feel the hatred build up inside. She would physically feel how much she hated her brother. She wished he were dead.

After work, she'd be drained. That split-second of reliving the memory and feeling all that anger would exhaust her, and she would go home to her safe, comforting world. She would slip into her comfy clothes, turn on the TV, and scroll through social media during the commercials. She didn't exercise.

Oftentimes, after a big day of work and feeling unseen by her husband, she would slip into the euphoria of eating an entire bag of her favorite chips. Chip after chip, she allowed herself to feel the pleasure of the taste until the bag was gone. The feeling of "fullness" in her belly would set in, and soon her attention wasn't on that pit in her stomach from her soul's nudgings. For a few minutes, she didn't have to wonder about her relationship with her husband. Did he see her? Did he even really love her?

She knew she would enjoy the full feeling for only about five minutes. Then the guilt would come in like a heavy fog, and the not-so-friendly voice would rage.

You are so pathetic.

You just ate a whole bag of chips.

That bag of chips could have fed a family picnic.

You're fat.

You don't even work out and you know you should.

Your husband doesn't love you, but why should he? You just ate a whole bag of chips and you have crumbs all over your shirt.

On and on it would go.

One day she would feel a surge of inspiration to exercise. To take back her life. To release the extra weight. To feel energized. To feel hope. She would turn on her favorite music and a video of her favorite trainer, and about five minutes in—with her heart pumping, blood surging through her veins—she would *feel*. Her heart would race, not because she was out of breath, but because she was starting to feel her emotions, even though she didn't want to. Feeling would mean remembering for longer than a few seconds. She quickly told herself working out was too hard for her. She was too out of shape, too old for this type of movement.

Months later she found out that the pit in her stomach about her husband was there for a reason. He had a secret of his own. In her mind, he was a sex addict and he had been cheating on her for years.

Talking Your Way through It

Now, this dialogue I'm going to share with you may seem simple. The actual conversation was only about 30 minutes long, but this is truly how fast she was able to release and forgive. She was finally willing to do the work. She was willing to get vulnerable. She was willing to use her voice. She fought for her freedom—and she won.

Molly: "I hate my life. I hate my brother. I hate my husband. I probably attracted this type of relationship. Of course I would marry a sex addict."

Me: "Yes, you did attract this. Your pain is not healed, so the Universe brought you more pain that resembled the pain you were already feeling in your subconscious and in your conscious. Let's go back to what happened to you. Yes, it was horrible. Yes, it is not excusable. Why haven't you shared this until now?"

Molly: "Afraid. Embarrassed."

Me: "How does it feel to share?"

Molly: "Better, but I am still angry. I still hate my brother. I still wish he were dead."

Me: "Can you forgive him?"

Molly: "No."

Me: "Is your brother abusing you right now? Will your brother be able to abuse you tomorrow or in the future? Are you safe from him?"

Molly: "My brother is not abusing me now. It happened thirty years ago. No, he is not abusing me in the future. And, yes, I am safe right now."

Me: "So one moment in time, even though it was horrible, is still dictating your life? Is it consuming your thoughts? Does it control what decisions you make or don't make? Is it directing your path? Are you still holding on to it? Where does it reside in your body?"

Molly: "Yes, I am still holding on to it, and, yes, I can see how it is dictating who I associate with, how much weight I am carrying. How much pain I am shoving down. It resides in my heart and my mind."

Me: "So we realize that you are safe; this is not happening to you now. But you are allowing your story to run the show. You are allowing the story to play out in your mind. This story is running your choices, your direction in life. Can you forgive your brother, so you can be free? You are giving your offender power every day. You wishing he would die is like drinking poison and hoping your enemy will die. *You* are carrying this. Forgiveness is not about making what happened okay, or right, or sweeping over it. Forgiveness is your gift to yourself so you no longer give your offender power. You no longer inflict poison on your life. Forgiveness is saying, 'I forgive you . . . so I can be free. I forgive myself for holding on to this belief that I am not enough. That I somehow deserved this. I forgive the girl who felt pain and then inflicted that pain on herself every single day for thirty years, reliving it and feeling it every single day.' Molly, can you forgive your brother?"

Molly: "Yes."

As she broke down sobbing, I could feel the energy shift as her shoulders slumped forward. All the emotion she had caged up within her was seeping out.

Later, Molly and I unlayered that she put on weight subconsciously to protect herself from sexual abuse. She didn't want to be too sexy or desired ever again. She realized she didn't work out because moving her body tapped into her soul. It made her feel. It was trying to heal her, but her ego would shut it out over and over again.

Through forgiveness for her brother, and, more important, for herself, she has released her husband, she has released weight, she has stepped in to *feeling* through healing foods and healing movement, and she chooses each day to say healing words to her spirit. To speak the grace that is the truth to her soul: "I am enough. I have always been enough. I am worthy of love."

There are vital steps and understandings toward forgiveness for yourself and your offender:

1. Speak your story. Speaking it doesn't make it bigger or messier. Speaking it gives your truth a voice. Speaking it is the first step to your healing. Speaking releases the chains it has around your heart, throat, and body.

2. Recognize the hurt little girl or boy inside of you. Don't try to bypass their hurt, but recognize that what happened in the past is a story that you can either live in or step on.

3. Ask yourself, "Is this still happening to me today? Is this happening to me tomorrow or in the future?"

4. Ask yourself if you are allowing one moment in time to dictate your life. What about your choices, your energy, and the people you allow or don't allow in your life?

5. Ask yourself, "Am I willing to forgive? Am I willing to forgive the perceptions that were taken on with the pain that I have allowed to sweep through my soul? Am I willing to forgive myself and my offender?"

Remember, forgiveness does not mean you are saying, "What has happened is okay." It means you are freeing yourself energetically from the person who hurt you. You are removing their power from your heart. You have the power to break the heavy chains of relationships that no longer serve your higher self. You can free yourself to focus on all the good currently in your life, and what you are creating moving forward.

Forgiveness opens you to unlimited possibilities energetically. That's the amazing thing—you don't have to exchange words or write a letter or have anything to do with the person you're forgiving. All that needs to occur takes place within *you*, and the rest of it works itself out in the cosmos.*

Even if the other person hasn't forgiven you, that is okay. That doesn't really matter. What matters more is about you and your process and what you know *you* have forgiven. There is a freedom in that, and that freedom lies in knowing that you can take any bad situation and turn it into something beautiful. When I found it within my heart to forgive Laerer and my father, I was finally free to live in the present moment—which is the *only* way we can truly live.

Who do you need to forgive to feel free?

What would it feel like to be free and allow forgiveness to sweep over all of your life?

Where in your relationships can you respond with grace instead of anger or disappointment?

CHAPTER 8

My Tribe of Sisters

Surround yourself with people who make you hungry for life, touch your heart, and nourish your soul.

— Unknown

I was always somewhat of a tomboy. In school, I ran track and played volleyball and basketball. Most of the girls on the basketball team made fun of the cheerleaders, and when we were freshmen, a group of five of us made a bet that we would all try out for the cheerleading team our senior year as a joke. None of us took the tryouts seriously. We were being complete goofballs, screaming and doing big jumps and kicks. We thought we were *so funny*, and I'm sure we were being completely disrespectful, though I was too young to think of it that way at the time. But the next day, my name was on the list of those who made it, along with one other girl from our group.

I tried to get out of it, but my friends held me to it. As uncomfortable as I was about it then, I am actually thankful for that experience because it made me swallow my pride. It also made me work really hard! Cheerleading was not nearly as easy as I'd originally thought—I was a terrible dancer, and since I wasn't used to this kind of thing, it was hard for me to learn the cheers. I had to get up early and practice for an hour before school and an hour after school just to get by without being ridiculed on game nights.

As I spent more time with the squad, I was appalled by how catty these particular girls were. These cheerleaders hung out with each other, had sleepovers, and proclaimed they were best friends, and yet they were always saying mean things about each other and gossiping behind one another's back. It didn't make any sense to me to be unkind to someone you liked.

I never really had an example of true female friendship, from either the cheerleading squad or the basketball team. While my teenage friends from basketball and track weren't catty, they also weren't necessarily the type of girls who were there for you to share your deep, dark, exciting secrets with and be completely vulnerable around. There was always the element of competitiveness that comes along with sports, so I never really had a true, deep friend who would have my back at any cost.

Deep down, I always wanted a raw, deep, fun friendship. I didn't know if having this type of true friend was in my future, so I pretended that I didn't need that type of friend. It was safer to pretend that I was a tomboy and didn't need girlfriends. That way I couldn't get hurt. I held on to that lie all through college, and even my entire adult life, until my Year of Divine Awakening.

Leaps of Faith

I was going through my hardest time—I'd lost my son, was going through an unpleasant divorce, and was living in a new town, which was very religious. I felt isolated from my community and my parents. I was alone and longed for companionship, but was too scared to reach out to anyone. And that's when I received the unexpected gift of true friendship.

D. came into my life when I wasn't looking for a friend. She had heard about the divorce and she'd had a similar experience. Instead of avoiding me, like I felt many people did at that time, she got my number and reached out to me now and then, asking how I was doing and if I needed anything.

I was reluctant to respond with anything more than a brief message, since I didn't know her at all and wasn't sure what her motive might be. Her motive, as it turned out, was absolutely pure. She could sense that I was struggling and knew firsthand that it was not a popular decision to divorce the "nice guy," especially in a small religious town. She also gave me the benefit of the doubt and thought there could be more to the rumors that were being spread about me.

What finally convinced me to connect with her is when she invited me to her community pool where my kids could swim with her kids. Being a single mom now, anything I could do to get my kids busy and take their minds off of our new reality was a welcome relief. Once I met D. face-to-face I felt her kindness and I felt comfortable enough to begin to talk to her about what was going on. And that was the beginning of a deep friendship.

She supported me in business by joining my online fitness challenge and offered me business advice, deep friendship, and trust. I finally had a deep connection with someone who didn't judge me, who loved me with all my flaws, and who was a good friend. Since neither of us had biological sisters, we were able to experience this new sisterhood together—what we imagined sisters do, how they show up for each other, what kind of conversations they have. We knew the worst about each other and we continued to push one another to be our best.

Some of our best moments together, as busy moms, were when we could get up at 5 A.M. when our kids were sleeping, strap on our boots, grab our headlamps, pick up coffee, and go hike up the local mountain—rain, shine, or snow. We had deep conversations on these hikes. I was allowed to share my biggest dreams and my lowest of lows without judgment, and she was able to do the same. That was such a grounding place for me, and it allowed me to spread my wings and start to soar. She was the first person who truly showed me what was possible in a friend, in true sisterhood.

About a year into my friendship with D.—with hundreds of hikes to bond us together—Craig and I moved to Vail. Craig and I had gotten married there, and it was where Craig was from. The distance from D. created a massive void in my life. I missed her like crazy. I missed our daily coffee walks, the belly laughs, and the honest conversations.

At that point, I was checking off the steps toward my mission: growing my financial abundance, having a loving relationship with my husband, and cultivating my relationship with my girls. I was checking off good times, traveling, and stepping into my soul's nudgings. I was doing the deep internal work of forgiveness, stepping into my own spirituality and truth. The one missing piece was having a tribe of friends. But now I knew creating new friendships was possible.

Even with Craig as my new business partner and husband, I was actually quite lonely. Craig was and is my best friend, but to expect one person in your life to fulfill you in everything and act as your sounding board in all areas is a huge disservice to them as well as yourself.

All the mentors in my life talked about the importance of a tribe, one that supported you and cheered you on, that helped you see your blind spots and the depths of who you are. I wanted to be seen for who I was, lifted and elevated into my true potential, and I wanted to do that for others.

After I read in Jack Canfield's book *The Success Principles* about how to create a mastermind group and how it could help catapult you in both your personal life and your business, I meditated on the idea of a mastermind and the names of two women popped into my head to reach out to. I knew a little about what they did, but we had not shared more than one conversation each, and they didn't know each other at all.

Lori is a fitness professional whom I had met back when I did the bikini competition; she was well-known in those circles for having won Fitness Universe. She shares my passion for healing foods and elevating women's lives, and I could tell she had a very similar business model and mission to mine, but that bikini competition felt like a lifetime ago.

Lindsay is a transformation coach, and the mother of four beautiful children. We met on my first trip to Costa Rica. I kept on running into her—at the beach, at restaurants, and on the streets. I knew if I kept seeing someone that often, there was a reason we were supposed to meet. She felt the same way, so we had a smoothie together and connected for about an hour. I don't even remember anything we talked about! I just remember feeling deep in my cells that I would somehow be working with this woman or be connected to her in some way in the future. But we lost contact after that trip.

Given all the distance, I had to question whether this was really a good idea. Frankly, I was terrified to reach out. But I knew that if I received a mental download of information during meditation, I needed to act on it.

I had Lori's number and Lindsay's e-mail. I told each about my vision for a mastermind, that I'd meditated on it, and that their names had come up. Then I asked if they'd be interested in forming a mastermind group with one other woman that would meet twice a month. Both said yes.

I laid out the ground rules on the first call:

1. We would meet at a specific day and time, and we would not go over the time allotted. (We set an hour for our calls and met twice a month, every other week.) The magic number for a mastermind group is three to five people, especially if you set an hour, because that gives everyone time to share.

2. Before we shared, we would begin with a prayer from the leader, setting the stage and intention for that call. The leader position would rotate with each call.

3. We would be willing to be raw and vulnerable, asking for what we needed help with and willing to help each other 100 percent. If one of us said we needed help in any area, the other two would give 100 percent of their knowledge, support, and advice. Everything that was said on those calls was sacred and not to be shared with anyone outside the group.

We spent that first call getting to know each other—but it wasn't small talk. I shared things I'd never shared, and they shared deeply, too. As the calls continued, we were able to dig into business struggles, manifesting dreams, family dynamics, deep fears, and our most audacious goals. We supported each other 100 percent.

Almost immediately, all the dreams we were sharing together began manifesting! Each one of us started retreats and events, developed our coaching practices, wrote books, deepened our personal relationships, and grew leaps and bounds in all areas of our lives through this support, love, and raw vulnerability.

We've all three stayed committed to our mastermind group, even when we travel. We'll sacrifice sleep and have calls in the middle of the night to make sure we honor the group and honor the commitment we've made to each other. We are there to lift each other up in the very lowest times of our lives, reminding each other of our strength, our courage, and our mission. And we are celebrating our highs and our greatest successes without comparison or jealousy—just real, authentic excitement and love for the other.

It feels so good to experience the deep, grounded feeling when you know you have sisters who have your back. You know that no matter what happens, you have someone who will be there for you in your lowest of lows. On a deep cellular level, this knowing gives you the courage to fly as high as you're meant to fly. These women will hold you to the truth of your soul and shine the light when you are in deep darkness.

When I experienced the downfall of divorce, I had to confront my own lack of support—if something were to crumble in my relationship, who do I have to catch me? I learned the hard way that my parents might not be there.

I now know that I will always have these women. It took commitment, determination, and getting way out of my comfort zone to reach out to them. But I wouldn't trade my sisters for the world.

True sisters have a deep connection and deep love for one another. They support you as you share all those wild, courageous dreams, and they hold you to a higher standard of your soul's remembrance to implement them.

THE POWER OF SISTERHOOD

A few years ago, I was leading a retreat with Lindsay in Costa Rica. One day, we were having a moment with Lori, sitting in a sacred triangle with our knees touching, drinking kombucha and eating raw cacao. We decided on this day to go one step deeper, to share the shadows that we've always been afraid to share, the areas in our own lives where we can be sneaky and hide—and we would share the shadows that we see in each other.

It was scary to say, "I'm willing to hear what you have to say about me, and I receive it." For me, it unlayered the part of me that feels that unless I'm in action, I'm not doing enough—or I *am not* enough. Lindsay and Lori reminded me that sometimes I made myself busy to cover up the need to be seen or the feeling that I was not enough. That maybe I was afraid of not feeling enough if I spent time just *being* instead of *doing*. That message, delivered in deep trust and love, was profound for my personal growth.

We all shared, and we were all able to cry, look into each other's eyes, and say, "Hey, it's okay. I've got your back. I'm here for you. I love you." We celebrate the dirt in each other's lives as much as the victories.

The time I started developing these deep connections with other women coincided with the time I set up my online tribe of women in my programs. I set my intention around what I wanted for others: loving, nonjudgmental, encouraging relationships. I didn't want any other woman to feel how I felt, feeling alone while going through the hard times and never really having a sister to turn to. We were very careful to create a platform and programs with built-in intentionality, where women would be nurtured and encouraged and no woman would feel alone. I wanted to create a worldwide sisterhood where women came together under one universal principle—the willingness to step into radical self-love and unlayering through healing foods, a healing mind-set, and healing movement.

And, sure enough, I began witnessing sisters reaching out to one another in love in our private Facebook group "Fit Rise Tribe" from all around the globe. Every single one of these women in the Facebook group* has stepped into this program because they're willing to say loving words, try healthy foods, and move their bodies in love regularly. No matter who these women are—their politics, how they raise their kids, their culture, their location, their religious beliefs—we all have this fundamental common denominator: We want to be in the full expression of who we are. We want to be seen. We choose to see one another's spirits. And we are willing to do the work.

These women have become best friends online.* When one woman is courageous and shares her before and after pictures while standing in her kitchen, or shares her truth that she wants to lose 100 pounds, thousands of women celebrate her and surround her with positive messages of love and encouragement. They hold her accountable with love and remind her that she is worthy and beautiful and powerful.

I tear up every single time I see these acts of love, because I know many of these women don't have that same support in their daily lives and wouldn't dare share pictures with their friends and family. But here, they gets thousands of comments of support and thousands of likes! That much support allows them to soar.

Every woman wants to be seen and celebrated. She wants to be held, and to have deep, electrifying, raw, truth-telling conversations. I know it can feel like it is a hard relationship to find. I've been there! If you are missing that connection in your life, you can begin to call it in through meditation and intention, just as I did. At times, that loving sister gets placed in your life, like a surprise gift, like D. was for me, but most often, you have to create it and then cultivate it. Whenever you feel an inspiration to call someone, reach out to someone, or set up something, you must act and you must act immediately, because if you don't, you will talk yourself out of it.

I isolated myself from women for so long out of fear of being judged and not accepted, and I never want another woman to feel that kind of loneliness.

A tribe of loving sisters really is out there, just waiting for you to create it!

You are meant to Rise within and shine so bright that you light up every corner of the room and every corner of the world—you can even light up a corner for a woman in the dark who can't see her own light. That's what this is about.

We are all connected and we always have been. Divine sisters have your back and they will walk with you because there is a deep cellular remembering, from the beginning of time and down through the ages, of these words: "I promised to walk with you. Here, take my hand."

True sisterhood is being seen for who you are, not the makeup or clothes you are wearing, the beliefs you carry, or the kind of mom you are. Sisterhood grounds us so our growth can accelerate. And as a side bonus, the pressure is taken off our primary relationship, should we have one, because our husbands or partners don't have to be all things to us; we have others to turn to.

Due to this friendship, I feel like everything is coming at me at warp speed. A tribe does not have to be made up of blood relatives. My tribe is my "chosen family." I get to choose who I surround myself with, and I get to create my village of support.

Creating a tribe of sisters is an intentional process of hand-selecting the people you want to share your energy with. Energy is sacred. Time is sacred. Life is sacred. And the deep bond of sisterhood is sacred. When making your selections, be clear on what you are calling into your space. Surround yourself with women who light you up. Women who will be there to both celebrate your wins and hold you in times of despair. Women around whom you can be authentically yourself. Women who hold you to a high standard and won't let you settle for mediocrity in your life.

Our sisters are the wind in our sails so we can travel farther and fly higher. With the support of our sisters, we have the silent push of courage to go after our dreams. So find your sisters, create your tribe, and experience the beauty of unconditional love, support, and connection.

What type of sisterhood do you want to create in your life?

What does being a great friend mean to you?

Where in your life could you be a greater friend?

CHAPTER 9

Honoring My Soul Every Single Time

Courage starts with showing up and letting ourselves be seen.

—BRENÉ BROWN

We've been talking about soul nudgings and how sometimes they're more like soul *shouts*. But other times, those nudgings are softer, gentler. They don't present themselves as fear or emotional breakdowns or physical breakdowns; instead, these soul nudgings show up as curiosity.

Sometimes this curiosity can lead you to experiences and understanding you never expected. While I was leading retreats in Costa Rica, I met another traditional healer, someone who was said to be completely transformational. I was skeptical, because hey, I didn't know the guy, but I was also curious.

I decided to take seven days of deep immersion with his teachings in the jungle of Costa Rica. From San José, we drove for hours in silence through the lush, rolling mountains, and then we went even farther, taking a boat to a remote island. There was no Wi-Fi, and we were going to be sleeping in a hut on stilts, right on the ocean. This was either going to be the makings of a perfect murder or a beautiful experience.

The healer began by teaching me about the different types of modalities of healing that crossed over from different countries. He talked about how each muscle group in the body holds a specific emotion: Love is in the glutes, fear is in the lats and back, and safety is in the abdomen. I was taking all of this in, making copious amounts of notes, when he stopped suddenly and said, "We need to work on your self-love."

This was not what I had been looking for. I wanted to learn about these different forms of healing—I did *not* want those lessons turned back on me. But he was gentle with me. We started with a simple conversation; I talked about my life, my past. He explained that so many women need more self-love, and that if I was going to be a healer—a teacher—I would need to be able to own my love for my self so that I could help other women do the same.

THE FIRST LESSON IN SELF-LOVE

While I was able to understand and connect with his message mentally, my physical body was going haywire, trying to process what was really going on. As my time with this healer went on, my skin started to break out. White, pus-filled, inflamed zits were popping up all over my chin, neck, and mouth. I wasn't eating anything abnormal, only natural, healing foods, so there was no reason this should be happening to my skin. I'd had breakouts with acne in the past, but nothing like this. My skin was treacherous, with big red boils erupting overnight.

There was only one small mirror on the whole property. By the afternoon of day three, I looked into it and thought, *Oh, my gosh, I look hideous!* I went and got my makeup bag and started to put some tinted moisturizer on.

As soon as I opened the cap to my makeup, my teacher came around the corner. In such a loving way, as if he were Buddha, he said, "Why are you covering up your face?"

"I want to put sunscreen on." I totally lied, because I was supposed to be on this self-love journey, right?

"Don't cover your skin. It is beautiful." *What? Have you seen my face?*

He walked to a tree and came back with a piece of fruit in his hand. It had bumps and blemishes all over it.

"This fruit is some of the most powerful fruit you can ever eat," he said. "It has so many healing properties. See these blemishes on this fruit? It is just like your skin, but the fruit totally accepts the blemishes. It shows up in its healing power despite what is covering its skin. It is time for you to accept your skin. Your body is just talking to you. When are you going to accept every blemish and every beauty mark and every piece of you?

"You are beautiful and you have many things you need to deliver to the world, many things inside of you. You cannot let the blemishes stop you. They are part of your growth."

I knew, of course, that my body could send me messages. But it was something else entirely to *accept* those messages—and to be all right with having them displayed on my face for everyone to see.

The Second Lesson in Self-Love

I still had a long way to go. That afternoon, I developed a tickle in my throat that would not go away, no matter how much water I drank. I started coughing every 15 seconds. I knew I wasn't getting sick, so I wasn't sure what was happening. But my teacher knew.

Our huts only had thin wood walls. If anyone coughed or said anything, everyone would hear. My coughing fit continued through dinner and lasted all night. My teacher came to me, gently asking, "Are you okay?" I nodded yes. I wasn't dying or anything, though it probably sounded like it! I was so embarrassed. I knew I was keeping him awake. But he checked on me several times that night, without a shred of frustration. He said, "Your body is trying to talk to you. You are not using your voice."

He explained that my soul had a lot to say, but from years of not using my voice, and perhaps from ancient patterns passed on in my DNA from ancestors, I was not fully expressing my soul's call. I was hiding from my feminine power—quieting my voice, so I wouldn't offend anyone. My breakout and my coughing were my body's way of letting me know that *I am enough*. My soul was nudging me to stick up for myself, to use my voice, and to be my greatest friend.

The Third Lesson in Self-Love

Lesson three came through sandwork; it was about both letting go and being in the moment.

I knew that I was in Costa Rica, on a beach (which I *loved*), and I had chosen to be there, but I had never much liked the feeling of sand sticking to my body, especially if I was hot and sweaty. Of course, my teacher took me out to the sand to work out. We did some shamanic yoga, and in the humidity and the heat, I began dripping sweat.

When we finished, he said, "Sit down in the sand."

That was not at all appealing. "Actually, I'm good," I said. "Do you think we can meditate back on the grass?" I explained my sensory issues with sweat and sand.

"Lie down," he said.

He started to bury me in the sand. "What are you running away from? The sand is just another experience for you. It is just an irritant that you are trying to push out. But what if you embrace it? What if you just sit with it and let it go from an irritant to feeling good?"

Oh my gosh. This guy has lost his brains.

He could obviously sense my displeasure. I am not known for my poker face. But he continued telling me to surrender as the sand was now all the way over my torso and legs, with just my neck and head uncovered.

I *hate* that feeling of being held down. But I knew what he was trying to show me . . . so I let go. Soon the irritation went away and I could feel the coolness of the sand. I started to relax. It felt like a cool blanket. I didn't have to go anywhere or do anything. *What was I trying to get away from?*

When I accepted that sense of peace, I finally uncovered myself. By choosing to sit in my discomfort and staying in it a bit longer, I learned I was able to push through experiences that were unpleasant. More than that, I learned that I could transmute those experiences and turn them into something positive, even empowering. There were so many places in my life where I could stop running from that kind of discomfort—confrontations in business, addressing friendships that were no longer serving me, setting boundaries. The list was endless. I couldn't wait to see how this lesson could be applied even more in my life.

The Fourth Lesson in Self-Love

I experienced my fourth lesson while on a hike.

The trail was filled with lush vegetation on either side. When we got to the top of the trail, the healer pulled out a ceremonial cup with a chocolate drink in it. I understood that we were about to have a sacred cacao ceremony. I knew that several tribes around the world performed cacao ceremonies every day, but I wasn't quite sure what that entailed.

We sat cross-legged with other locals in a circle. We each received a small ceramic cup. It was filled with rich, dark, raw cacao. We each went around the circle, infusing our cacao drinks with our love, our intentions, our gratitude for life—for abundance and for the *now* of this moment. As we sipped this divine, delicious elixir, I was filled with immense love. I felt grounded in my essence. I felt warmth, peace, and deep love penetrate my heart.

This ritual was so simple, and yet so profound. It was a celebration of pleasure and self-love, honoring my time, my body, my thoughts, and my life. We finished the ceremony with a deep meditation and then took a tour of the grounds. When I saw the cacao bean growing, suddenly I *knew* on a cellular level that I needed to bring this understanding of cacao into the mainstream.

So many of us love chocolate. Chocolate got its name from cacao, but the chocolate we eat today has been stripped of so much of what makes cacao so powerful. On a chemical level, cacao contains hundreds of healing properties, including anandamide, a fatty acid that is often referred to as the love drug. There are only two foods in the world that contain this molecule—cacao and black truffles. The molecule releases a chemical that stimulates bliss. Like caffeine, cacao has a direct conduit to the cells, but it doesn't provoke addiction or overstimulation. Instead, it helps with depression, mental focus, brain function, immunity, increasing feelings of love and acceptance, and so much more. It is one of the most powerful superfoods on the planet, and it just happens to be *delicious*.

As soon as I went home, my face instantly cleared up. That journey was a catalyst for me to own my self-love and step into more pleasure—and by owning my self-love journey, I was energetically allowing other women to do the same. Since that time, I've developed a line of cacao that is infused with a combination of other superfoods to enhance its healing properties and to heal individuals on a cellular level.*

Cacao is a tool for radical self-love. We can use it to induce pleasure, and in so doing, create a connection with *ourselves*, honoring the soul and our connection to Source. That connection, of course, is always there, but if we work with intention and use the tools we have available, we can get right down into our cells and speed up the process of learning to truly love ourselves, and not just feel but *listen* to our connection to Source.

SMOKE SIGNALS IN THE OZARKS

After my experiences in Costa Rica, I grew more curious about indigenous ways of living, indigenous ways of loving, and old ancient forms of healing. My curiosity took me all over the world, and one of my most powerful experiences was with a Native American healer named Arrow Hawk in the Ozark Mountains.

My family and I flew into Missouri and drove a rental car, winding through backcountry, passing small towns. When Google Maps said we'd finally arrived, we turned on to a red dirt road, where we saw teepees. We said hi to the others who were joining us for the weekend, arranged our teepee, and called it an early night. It had been a long day of traveling.

Sometime during the night, I was awakened by the sounds of Native American drumming and singing. I was a little disoriented, but my eyes were open, so I knew I wasn't dreaming. Our teepee was next to a dirt road and a fence, and I thought there must have been 20 people standing by the fence, drumming and singing. But that didn't make sense—there weren't many other people on the property besides Arrow Hawk, his family, and a few other people there for healing. This sounded like a lot more people than that.

At first I thought they were probably drumming and singing in the middle of the night as part of a welcoming ceremony. And then dogs started howling—way more dogs than the two who had greeted us when we pulled up.

Miraculously, the kids were still asleep. Even Craig, who is a super-light sleeper, was dreaming away. I closed my eyes and tried to go back to sleep, too—but I soon woke up again in a panic. I could not breathe; it felt like I was being choked from smoke. I said, "I can't get any air!"

Craig and my girls were still sound asleep, but I was angry and frightened for them. I was starting to hallucinate a bit, and I thought someone had to be outside of our teepee, wafting drugs into our tent. I nudged Craig and said, "I can't breathe!" He only rolled over. *My whole family has been drugged! They can't even wake up! As soon as the first light hits in the morning, we are out of here. I want nothing to do with this.*

Somehow I finally fell back to sleep. I woke at sunrise, ready to pack up and leave, but the girls were chipper and excited to go play with the cats and the dogs and tour the land and the teepees. My breathing was normal, so I asked the girls and Craig, "Are you guys okay? Did you have a hard time breathing last night?"

No, they all slept great.

I asked Craig quietly, "Did you feel like you were on drugs last night?" He didn't know what I was talking about. "You didn't hear them singing and drumming last night?" He shook his head no.

I knew *something* had happened. So I set off to find Arrow Hawk and give him a piece of my mind. But before I even got a word in, he said, "You were visited last night, weren't you?" It wasn't a question. He knew what had happened.

I said, "Did you do that? Were you guys out there singing last night?"

"No."

"Were there a bunch of dogs howling last night?"

"No. There are only two dogs on this property."

One of the men from the group walked by. He took a sip of his coffee and said, "I got up in the middle of the night to go to the bathroom and I don't know what you are talking about. There was nothing but stars and silence."

Arrow Hawk had a little glimmer in his eye. "You have been visited."

I lost it at that point. I started crying, telling him everything I'd experienced. He explained that he'd also been visited when he first moved on the land and that he had been scared to death. He said, "They were doing medicine work on you. You have to use your voice more. You are not sharing as much as you are supposed to be sharing and they were trying to communicate this to you. They are here to push you into your calling, to encourage you to step into your purpose here on this planet."

That was my first experience with the unseen world, but it wouldn't be the last. Every night after that, for three nights straight, I was visited in a different way. Each time, I would wake up, thinking I was dreaming, and still hear the sounds and feel the feelings of the experiences going on around me. I understood then that my soul resided in both the seen and the unseen worlds. It was an understanding that the unseen has its place in our reality. And it was yet another reminder to use my voice—just as I'd been encouraged to do in Costa Rica.

Mayan Lessons in Simplicity and Sexuality

I wanted to have an experience with a tribe that hadn't yet been marked by modern society, where they still actively lived their traditions. I felt so blessed to be invited to visit a Mayan tribe, and I spent time with a beautiful healer woman named Fernanda. Similar to the traditions of the Native Americans and other indigenous tribes, the Mayans used the power of sweat lodges called *temazcals* for cellular healing, emotional healing, and empowerment. These circular lodges are made of clay and dirt with at least one door facing the north. Before a ceremony, sacred lava rocks are heated and prepped with healing oils, plants, and herbs for hours. Once in the lodge, the lava rocks are carefully placed in the center, slowly heating up the lodge. Then you sit—with the heat, with the pressure of your life. The practice can help you to see hidden parts of your soul and illuminate your gifts, where you can lean in more in your life and see what you can strip away. By releasing sweat, we physically release toxins and energetically release what no longer serves us.

Fernanda taught me that women have been given the gift of being able to experience multiple orgasms in order to fuel our creative energy. I was pretty pleased with my ability to have *one* orgasm—and I think a lot of us are! But some women can have up to 15 at a time, if they set an intention to connect with the self, connect with their partner, and connect to Divine Source. In some cultures, men would line up for miles to hear the wisdom from women who had been connected to this higher power during the ecstatic state of orgasm.

Fernanda explained that it was customary in her culture, and in the ancient wisdom of some tribes, to receive pleasure and inspiration like this. They use it as a gift, to open the creative portal, allowing a deeper connection to divine wisdom—which can then deepen your ability to receive pleasure in all areas of your life. Fernanda encouraged me to tap into this sexual ability to have multiple orgasms, and to set the intention to see what came up during this surrender to pleasure.

Pleasure Is Your Divine Birthright

I was being pulled to surrender to the call of pleasure-seeking through many forms and by being present to all the gifts around me, especially to my sexual gifts. Talking about sex or sexual energy was a taboo conversation growing up. I believe it is indeed sacred. I believe it can be a direct conduit to God, the Universe, and Source.

However, I believe that full sexual expression requires a safe space and a safe partnership. If you are expressing with a partner, it needs to be someone who respects you, holds space for your expansion, and honors all of you.

After adopting this new mind-set around sex, my next sexual connection with Craig was eye-opening and created a deeper understanding of this power. We had already been having very satisfying sex, but I had no idea that this is what it could be like! On a very profound Tuesday, overlooking the ocean, after a leisurely aromatherapy soak in a big tub with bath salts, I was strewn over the white sheets, sun coming in, with the ocean's rhythmic waves breaking again and again in my sight. As I allowed my body to surrender, I was in full expression of the moment, going deeper and deeper within each movement.

I had released any thoughts of *Do I look good? Am I doing this right?* I was feeling only the ecstatic sensations within my body. I was able to release all tension, time, and restrictions. I gave myself permission to be in this vibration of pure pleasure, understanding that I am pure pleasure and that I am deserving of pure pleasure. Giving myself the grace and the time to be present with the sensations of my body, I was going higher and higher in my climax.

The beautiful man underneath me was a sacred portal for me to Rise, allowing me to climax with grace and stature. His patience allowed for this release and expression. He helped me realize the beautiful gift that we all have; in my pleasure, he receives pleasure, and in his patience, I receive grace. We're all connected in body, spirit, and mind. We're all one. As we connect with our body in divine pleasure, we then can see and manifest on the highest, grandest scale.

By allowing myself to be in full expression of my internal feelings and releasing any thoughts or limitations, I was able to go even deeper and my intention became even clearer. My connection to Source heightened, and it was deeper and more profound than I could ever imagine.

I understood on an even deeper level the importance of honoring the soul, even when it wasn't convenient, even if no one understood. I was committed to honoring me and what my soul wanted to experience through me. By tapping into more pleasure, I was able to use this force for creation and manifestation.

THE POWER OF SELF-LOVE AND PLEASURE

The journey of honoring my soul was taking me to places I never dreamed of. Over the next two years, I visited different healers in Mexico and Bali. I lived in Bali with my family, where we volunteered at several orphanages, shifting our perceptions and beliefs, and learning to love more and deeper with less. We lived in Costa Rica for three months, and we only brought 20 items each—including clothes and toys for the girls. We discovered that we were able to connect like never before since we had fewer belongings and fewer distractions to keep us pre-occupied. Nature became our playground, our dinner table, our candy shop, and our medicine cabinet.

I learned—and continue to learn—that everything we seek is within us. We are the teacher, the healer, and the lover. We can have greater peace in our body, heart, mind, and spirit. We can enjoy a better body, superior relationships, health, and wellness when we learn how to tap into the power of our mind, and use it to safeguard, heal, and restore all that life has damaged and thrown our way.

But in sharing my stories about healers I have visited and the divine insights and healing practices I gleaned, I want to make something abundantly clear: *There is no one outside of you who can know your soul, your path, or your heart better than you.* You are the guru. You have all the wisdom, all the inner knowings, inside of you.

I believe our souls nudge us to key information to remind us of our truth. They can direct us to certain people who can share with us knowledge we can use. But we already know in our souls everything we absolutely need to know about our own paths.

We are surrounded by information, but how can we discern if the knowledge we are being offered is correct or aligned with our truth? Trust in your own curiosity. Remember, your curiosity is your soul nudging you to investigate further. If, at that point, you read, see, or hear something that makes your heart light up, then that is a sign to go even deeper. Always trust your intuition—if, at any point, something doesn't feel right, pull back again. Even if every step of the way so far has proven to be perfectly aligned, the moment something *doesn't* feel true to you, pay attention.

You want to be wary of putting your power into someone else's hands. Always remember that no one can direct your path better than you can. No one has all the answers for *your* life.

Standing in your own self-love gives you the power to really *listen* to that self, and to speak for and from your soul.

Pleasure, in all its forms, is about connecting to Divine Source and to our own inner wisdom. Pleasure can be found everywhere we look, and in each moment—it isn't just sexual in nature. It can be found in the gentle breeze on a cold winter morning, the touch of a baby's chubby fingers, the smell of fresh laundry, the roughness of a tree's strong trunk, and the soft and wispy nature of aspen leaves. Pleasure allows us to step closer to Source, ground ourselves, and feel a sense of euphoria.

Mother Nature is our greatest healer. She wants us to play in the water. To stand in the dirt. To visit the jungle. To bury ourselves in the sand. Mother Nature can heal us and remind us of the core essence of who we are.

Mother Nature doesn't need saving. *She's here to save us.*

Where in your life can you receive more pleasure?

What is your soul trying to express in this lifetime?

What sets your heart on fire?

CHAPTER 10

The Rise

*Every woman who heals herself helps heal
all the women who came before her and
all those who will come after her.*

— DR. CHRISTIANE NORTHRUP

This is a time of a great awakening of our Divine Sisterhood. The vows of silence have been lifted. We, as a collective, are birthing a new age. Each one of us is part of this Divine Sisterhood, and by coming together and healing ourselves, we will bring about a much-needed shift on the planet and for humanity.

Since ancient times, silence has often been demanded of women; we couldn't speak up to share these gifts and truths that have always been boiling inside us without risking injury, shame, or even death. But now that shroud of silence is gone. The Divine Feminine is awakened and ready to Rise. We are slowly remembering the sacredness of what it means to be a woman.

It is time for us to allow what is beckoning and building within to be given the permission and space to Rise. And we can look to nature, as always, for a perfect example of the process and the beautiful outcome.

LESSONS FROM THE LOTUS

Revered in many cultures as a sign of hope, beauty, and personal strength, the sacred lotus begins its life in the mud. The seed falls into the water and is buried below, deep within the debris made of dead and decaying matter. It is there that it begins the journey of life. The lotus pulls nutrients from the muck in order to grow upward through the water's surface, facing the sun, unfolding with radiant and colorful beauty.

We grow like the lotus, in this ultimate Rise of our lives. Our greatest responsibility and contribution to humanity is our willingness to do the shadow work, to love ourselves in the now—in our current body and in our current relationships, even when it feels like muck. So many of us are running from our mud and muck—but if we are going to grow tall and strong, we must embrace our time as a seed, doing the work in the dark.

I know this work of self-healing is not easy. My own gifts wrapped in sandpaper were so painful, and my own struggles with forgiveness and self-love often required more strength than I thought I possessed. Self-healing requires us to sit with our darkness, the shadows and hardships of our lives. That is the hardest part—to do nothing but go into the shadow and feel it, see it, and pull the nutrients for your growth, your evolution, your beauty, your expression in this life, by working on your self-love.

That moment when you have looked at your darkness and owned it is called the gap. You are in the midst of the muck, but your life is not yet showing the fruits of your labor. Your stem hasn't grown above the water yet. Even you are having a hard time seeing your own growth. But, day by day, you are sucking in the nutrients. You are doing the daily work. You are stepping into forgiveness. You are stepping into radical truth-telling. You are getting radical with who you are spending time with and the words you are speaking, and you are drawing a line in the sand about how you will be treated and, most important, how you are going to treat yourself.

Then, one day, you bloom. This is the expression phase, where the flow is. You are taking in the sun and reaping your harvest. You, and everyone around you, can see and appreciate how far you've come. You are taking in pleasure and living out your destiny and purpose—unashamed, uncovered, and unafraid of the elements.

I shared my stories, my muck, to give others permission to tell the truth in their own lives—and to shine, knowing they are enough. I had to unleash and eradicate my poverty story, my relationship story, my self-love story, and my self-worth story in order to get to where I am today. My success has very little to do with me just getting smarter or reading more books. It has everything to do with diving into my shadow work and recognizing that I had created my own reality, and I was capable of creating a new reality of redemption and growth and happiness!

You can do the exact same thing. Each story shared and released creates more nutrients for your growth. We need the mud and the muck so that we can grow into our fullest potential. We need the foundation to stand steady on our truth and our forgiveness, and Rise.

All the change we want to see accomplished on the planet requires us to do the deep work of self-love within our internal shadows. Once we are willing to do that, we can manifest and create the life of our dreams. Once we own that we are the change that we want to see in the world, miracles can happen.

Each of us has a calling, to Rise within ourselves, to shed what no longer serves us, and to claim our divine birthright and our happiness. As we each step into this willingness to Rise within, we create a chain reaction of radical, fiery, all-consuming self-love, and give others permission to do the same.

OUR COLLECTIVE ENERGY

Every woman is absolutely beautiful, and I believe it is time to fiercely reject anything that suggests otherwise.

The biggest calamity in our society is not global warming or wars or destruction—although those terrors cannot and should not be ignored. I believe the biggest calamity we face is this thick blanket of self-judgment and self-hate that we have smothered ourselves with for generations. It manifests in feeling like you are not enough, in remaining blind to your divine energy and capacity. This self-hate is creating the destruction that we see in the world. I believe that this lack of love is our biggest downfall and is therefore our greatest opportunity for change.

Remember that everything has its polar opposite; when we see massive calamity, there is also massive light. In every area of darkness, there are those beautiful beings who operate in love and in a space of complete responsibility for themselves and their emotions. They are called to radical truth-telling and radical self-love, and they are doing the work every single day. They are our examples that it can be done and our encouragement when the path is dark and uncertain. It is *your turn* to join in, to shine, to burn so brightly with self-love and manifestation that you can't help but light the way for others in times of doubt.

We each have power within us. We each have genius. It is time to unleash that internal knowing, that cellular remembrance, and it is time to stand in it, stand on top of it, and to proclaim what your soul is wanting to express in this life.

The greatest contribution you can make in your life, on this planet, is stepping into radical self-love—seeing yourself and loving all the different dimensions of who you are. To love other women in all of their dimensions, in all the ways they show up. When we operate from a place of complete love for ourselves and each other, we make better choices, choices that impact the entire world. We shift the energy of the planet, bringing more abundance, more acceptance, and less separation.

Self-love is both courageous and admirable. It is possible. It is necessary.

And it is time.

THE RISE

Women do not need to be taught. We awaken.

Every woman is born with a force within her, with mysterious powers of knowing, and ancient wisdom is always whispering, sharing truths to guide her. This rhythmic flow connects us to the life force of the planet and to the entire Universe.

We have spent far too long trying to fit into the role of the masculine, operating in timelines, operating in drive mode, shutting emotions out, and putting our dreams and desires in a box, living only slivers of life at a time. It is time that we open that box and step outside of it. It is time to move our hips, sway, call in nature, howl at the moon, get quiet, hear the whisperings from ancient times, and hear our ancestors. It is time to *remember*.

There is an awakening. A remembering of the sacredness of what it means to be a woman. It is time for us to allow what is beckoning within to be given the permission and space to Rise. It is time to unleash that internal knowing written in our souls. It is time to proclaim all that our souls want to express.

My Invitation

I take a stand for unconditional love.

I believe that life is abundant, a gift overflowing with choices and opportunities. We have opportunities to step into our superpowers and unleash our genius, experiencing exquisite happiness and making the contributions we are destined to make.

I dream of a world in which each sister and brother looks each other in the eye and sees the beauty of unconditional love, both for the other and for themselves. I dream of a world in which this love empowers all beings to step fully into the role they are here to play, raising the vibration of the planet to one of radical self-love.

This is a call for every woman to step into her shadows, to step into her truths, to own her life with 100 percent responsibility, and to do the work of self-love.

In doing so, we Rise, and we change the world.

RESOURCES

Get Your Free Gifts

Throughout this book, I've offered you free gifts to begin the journey of your own personal Rise. These gifts include . . .

- Free Healing Workouts: I want you to experience what a fun, energizing, healing workout feels like! Try two of my most popular 10-minute, full-body workouts!

- Free Healing Meal Plan and Detox: My fans love this meal plan! Try it out for one day and you'll see what true healing feels like.

- Free Healing Meditations: Meditations are a powerful tool for transformation. That's why I'm also giving you my favorite meditation to expand your self-love and start feeling great right away.

Please visit www.RiseGifts.com now to access all these free gifts.

Join the Fit Rise Tribe

During my own Rise, I discovered that the key that changed everything for me was simply focusing on healing foods, healing movements, and a healing mind-set. That's why I've created the Fit Rise community. This community encompasses everything I teach so you never have to worry about any other method of eating healthy, exercising regularly, or even personal growth. We've done it all for you!

Please visit www.TheRiseBook.com/FitRise
to join our amazing community.

Experience Superfood Healing Chocolate

Cacao Bliss is an exclusive blend of raw Peruvian cacao powder infused with high-powered superfoods designed to help you beat your cravings and give your body the nutrients it needs to keep you healthy, trim, and energized.

Its rich, decadent flavor, combined with its ability to heal your body, makes for a one-of-a-kind treat you'll enjoy on a daily basis.

Please visit www.TheRiseBook.com/Cacao to try this delicious, superfood healing chocolate for yourself.

Follow Danette for Inspiration and More Freebies

Facebook.com/TheDanetteMay

@DanetteMay

@TheDanetteMay

Website: danettemay.com

ENDNOTES

1. Gaétan Chevalier et al., "Earthing: Health Implications of Reconnecting the Human Body to the Earth's Surface Electrons," *Journal of Environmental and Public Health* (2012). https://www.hindawi.com/journals/jeph/2012/291541.

2. Andrew Newberg, M.D., and Mark Robert Waldman, *Words Can Change Your Brain: 12 Conversation Strategies to Build Trust, Resolve Conflict, and Increase Intimacy* (New York: Hudson Street Press, 2012), 3.

3. Ibid., 25–35.

ACKNOWLEDGMENTS

To me this section is one of the most profound. It is the honoring of all those who helped me in my Rise. Who show up not only for me, but for countless others. Who love no matter what.

For My Creator, my God, my Source. I have not walked a day wondering if I was loved by you. You were there in my falls and tears and in my greatest joys. You are my eternal, everlasting friend and the one I honor.

For All the women before me. Especially the women who stood up and proclaimed their truths when it wasn't popular. Who were vulnerable and honored their soul's expression above all else. Your strength and resilience have given me permission to do the same.

For Mother Earth. You show me the way every day. You are my gift, my courage, my answers, my strength.

For Sarah and Samantha. Being your mother during this time on earth is my greatest honor and my most noblest mission. You teach me more than any book could or has.

For Craig. You are my earth Angel . . . my best friend, my dreaming partner, my passionate lover. My safe place to land.

For Mom and Dad. Your deep love for us kids was felt. Thank you for the homemade Barbie house, barnyard animals, brutal honesty, and teaching of work ethic.

For the Hay House family. Thank you for believing in me and for impacting so many lives with the vision you cast. I feel honored being in this family.

For Reid Tracy. Your humbleness and kind heart is seen, and thank you for seeing me.

For Nikki and Alice. You're book editing ninjas with your depth and willingness to go there with me. And for holding me to my vision throughout this process.

For Darien. For giving me the deep profound feelings of loving a friend. I have loved you like none other.

For Lindsay and Lori. For reminding me of my truth. For the hour-long talks and the unwavering support. Through your love, I have felt so held, such that I can extend my wings and fly as high as I am meant to.

For Maya. For the belly laughs, deep ancient friendship, and doing the "work" with me.

For Shanna. For being my mirror in the mission. And walking it with me daily.

For Juanpa. For teaching me about ancient love and introducing me to my soul's call of bringing Raw Cacao to the world.

*For Elizabeth and Glenno*n. Your books and their raw truth between the pages gave me courage to share mine.

For my Mindful Health team. The mission is spread around the world because of each one of you.

For The Tribe Sisters. This book is written for each one of you. I have felt your prayers from all around the world. I have felt your heart and your support. This book is completely dedicated to you!!! May we All Rise. For as one Rises, we all Rise.

For All who have blessed my life. There are so many of you who have walked into my life at the right time, said the thing I needed to hear or feel the love that only you could express. Thank you for being the catalyst, the inspiration in my growth. There are so many of you . . . with each one fundamental in my Rise.

ABOUT THE AUTHOR

Danette May is a motivational speaker, best-selling author of several health and women's empowerment books, celebrity trainer, and mother. Danette is the founder of Mindful Health, LLC, and The Rise Movement. Danette stars in some of the top-selling fitness DVDs sold worldwide, is a top magazine model, and is a frequent guest on national TV, including *Access Hollywood*, Hallmark's *Home and Family*, and CBS.

Danette's own Rise began after losing her son during childbirth, getting divorced, and finding herself with $47 to her name. Then she decided to stop being a victim and rewrite her story. She began to focus on the three pillars of healing: healing foods, healing movement, and a healing mind-set.

These three pillars form the foundation of every program she has created since then. Danette has helped millions of people around the world step into radical self-love and a healthier body and mind. You can visit her online at: danettemay.com and facebook.com/thedanettemay.

Hay House Titles of Related Interest

Hay House Podcasts
Bring Fresh, Free Inspiration Each Week!

Hay House proudly offers a selection of life-changing audio content via our most popular podcasts!

Hay House Meditations Podcast

Features your favorite Hay House authors guiding you through meditations designed to help you relax and rejuvenate. Take their words into your soul and cruise through the week!

Dr. Wayne W. Dyer Podcast

Discover the timeless wisdom of Dr. Wayne W. Dyer, world-renowned spiritual teacher and affectionately known as "the father of motivation." Each week brings some of the best selections from the 10-year span of Dr. Dyer's talk show on HayHouseRadio.com.

Hay House World Summit Podcast

Over 1 million people from 217 countries and territories participate in the massive online event known as the Hay House World Summit. This podcast offers weekly mini-lessons from World Summits past as a taste of what you can hear during the annual event, which occurs each May.

Hay House Radio Podcast

Listen to some of the best moments from HayHouseRadio.com, featuring expert authors such as Dr. Christiane Northrup, Anthony William, Caroline Myss, James Van Praagh, and Doreen Virtue discussing topics such as health, self-healing, motivation, spirituality, positive psychology, and personal development.

Hay House Live Podcast

Enjoy a selection of insightful and inspiring lectures from Hay House Live, an exciting event series that features Hay House authors and leading experts in the fields of alternative health, nutrition, intuitive medicine, success, and more! Feel the electricity of our authors engaging with a live audience, and get motivated to live your best life possible!

Find Hay House podcasts on iTunes, or visit www.HayHouse.com/podcasts for more info.